C000298108

Behind the Scenes with Wainwright

At Harry Firth's retirement dinner in 1982 with wives. Reproduced courtesy of the *Westmorland Gazette*

Behind the Scenes with Wainwright

A Publisher's Perspective of a Reluctant Celebrity

By Andrew Nichol

KIRKLAND BOOKS

Kendal

2012

First published in 2012 by
Kirkland Books Limited
7 Smokehouse Yard
Stricklandgate
Kendal
Cumbria
LA9 4ND
United Kingdom
http://www.kirkland-books.biz
0800 8806247

1098765421

ISBN: 978-0-9572278-0-4

All royalties from the sale of this book will be donated to 'Macmillan
Caring Locally'.

© Copyright Andrew Nichol 2012

All rights are reserved. No part of this publication may be reproduced,
stored in a retrieval system or transmitted in any form or by any means,
electronic, mechanical, photocopying, recording or otherwise, without
prior permission of the publisher.

Printed by Titus Wilson, Kendal
2012
001.512

Foreword

ALMOST from the day I accepted responsibility for the general printing and book publishing departments of The Westmorland Gazette, people who were interested in Alfred Wainwright suggested I keep records and one day write a book. Although I had great admiration for AW and his writings, a book was not something I anticipated or intended. During one of our regular meetings only a few years prior to his death in June 1991, it was made abundantly clear to me by AW that he did not want anyone writing about him after his death, he did not want a memorial of any kind and his name was not to be linked with any commercial enterprise. Since that time, and for more than 20 years after his passing, I have respected those wishes, only proceeding with this book in response to the many requests for an authentic account of AW and events in which I was involved. As with all the Wainwright books published by The Westmorland Gazette, and by way of an apology to the 'Great Fellwanderer', it has been originated in Kendal and will be printed and published in Kendal.

Introduction

ALFRED Wainwright, or AW as I eventually came to know him, was born in Blackburn, in Lancashire, in 1907. After leaving school at the age of 13, he began working in the borough engineer's department in the town hall, transferring a few years later, against his wishes, to the borough treasurer's department. He was the youngest of four children and always remembered the hardships and poverty suffered by his mother in raising a young family on her own; his father, a stone mason by trade, was unemployed for long periods. As a youth he began to explore the countryside around Blackburn and produce his own maps. But a holiday he took in 1930 changed his life dramatically. He and a cousin came to the Lake District. The comparisons with life in the mill town, the beautiful scenery, the hills and lakes were later described by him as a 'coloured fairyland'. Their first expedition after travelling by bus through Kendal and arriving at Windermere was to go up Orrest Head, near Windermere Railway Station. The panorama which awaited their arrival at the top more than fulfilled his expectations. This was the day and the experience which were to lead to his leaving his home town and becoming one of the best known residents of the Lake District. His return home to Lancashire only served to feed his appetite to move away and 'live in a house with a garden'. His first marriage resulted in the tenancy of a council house and the birth of his only child, Peter. Further visits to the Lakes to explore new areas were taken as the opportunities arose. In 1941 he was accepted for the position as an assistant in Kendal borough treasurer's office and a council house was allocated, but this one had the advantage of a view of Kendal Castle. Life and outlook for AW had improved considerably. All the pleasures and beauties of the Lakes that he had experienced on that first holiday were now on his doorstep. His elevation to borough treasurer in 1947 was followed by the building of a house at the head of Kendal Green, with views over a wide range of fells. It was in the early 1950s that the idea of writing guide books to the Lakeland fells began to occupy his thoughts. After destroying the first dozen or more completed pages of Book One of his *Pictorial Guides*, he redesigned and rewrote the text and the book was published in 1955. The other six volumes took 11 years to complete and were published by The Westmorland Gazette, in Kendal, which was eventually to produce 50 of his manuscripts in total, with sales exceeding one million by the late 1980s.

And so began a collaboration between publisher and author which is a story of dreams-and-nightmares

It has never been my intention to write a book. I am not a writer or a journalist. Since leaving school at the age of 14, in 1946, I have always been employed in the newspaper trade but on the production side. After serving an apprenticeship as a compositor at the *Durham County Advertiser,* in Durham City, my various jobs took me to Darlington, Sunderland and Tamworth before finally taking up a position with The Westmorland Gazette, in Kendal, in 1969. Again it was on the production side and never at any time during my 23 years there did I anticipate the day would dawn when I would put pen to paper.

Without taking up too much time and space, I think a brief rundown of events which eventually brought me into contact with someone I had never heard of prior to coming to work at The Westmorland Gazette needs to be explained. Although originally my duties were purely on the newspaper side of the business, the name Wainwright was becoming familiar. To begin with, it was simply mentioned in connection with an occasional full-page advertisement in the Gazette for the Wainwright books. Other than that, there was always some aspect connected with his books, whether it be compositors making up the formes or chases of pages as they are known in the trade (formes or chases are steel frames used to hold pages in position during the printing process) or paper ready for printing, so be seen around the works. Pallets of printed sheets were stacked here and there in the machine room while in the bindery books in the various stages of finishing before going into the bookstore ready for packing and distribution.

After three years employed purely on the newspaper side of the business, I was asked by Bernard Fisher, the managing director at that time, if I would be prepared to take over production of the general printing in addition to that of the newspaper. The connection with Wainwright moved a step closer. However, it was still just a name - I had never met or even seen him. The books were something for the general printing staff to work on if there was nothing more urgent. Twice weekly, Monday afternoons at 2.30pm and Friday mornings at 10.30am, Harry Firth, the general printing manager, would put his head around the door and say: 'I'm off to see AW.'

Something was unusual about these Wainwright books - the typeface. Having worked in five different newspaper offices, I was familiar with quite a variety of different typefaces but not this one. It was unlike anything else I had ever previously come across and just assumed it was a typeface which had been made especially for these particular books. It did not occur to me that it was actually someone's handwriting. It was so consistent in so many ways. The line endings were in line or 'justified' as it is known in the trade.

Several months into the role of being responsible for the production of the newspaper and all aspects of general printing, including the Wainwright books, Harry Firth handed me a key and asked if I would find something from the filing cabinet in the cellar. As I searched for whatever it was I was looking for, the name Wainwright was about to take on a new meaning. Here in my hands were his original pages for the *Guide Books*. They were not produced from a typeface, they were handwritten. I couldn't quite believe what I was seeing. There must be another explanation - the consistency of the actual handwriting, the letter spacing, the word spacing, the line spacing, the justification of the line endings and, most remarkably, without the use of hyphens. I would not have thought it possible that someone could produce them freehand. I had been in the trade for more than 26 years but I had never come across anything like this. If they were in fact produced freehand, they must surely be classed as 'works of art'. Later, when I was able to raise the matter of the origination and Harry casually said they were all produced from AW's hand, I still could not understand why no-one seemed to think they were anything out of the ordinary. The name Wainwright certainly had taken on a new meaning.

Over the next ten years as works manager, I was Harry's right-hand man on the general printing together with my responsibilities for the production of the newspaper. The main activity and primary single source of income of the general printing department was the printing of the monthly magazines *Dalesman* and *Cumbria* which were published by the Dalesman Publishing Company of Clapham. The magazines were to be produced for publication at the beginning of each calendar month and were Harry's top priority. The Wainwright books were something to 'fall back on' when we were quiet.

Because the magazines were so important, if we were to remain competitive in both cost and quality, the money would have to be found to take advantage of the new printing technology which was changing and improving efficiency. The 'Wainwrights' were different. There was no typesetting. The origination was all by AW's hand - a printer's dream. The advantage with the new technology, known in the trade as offset printing, was that printing of the books, in flat sheet form, would be faster and of an improved quality than the old letterpress method.

A decision taken at higher level not to renew the magazines' printing contract prompted Harry to think in terms of retiring a year early, in June, 1982. When there was no mention of who was to replace him two weeks before his retirement date, I began to wonder if, due to the quite heavy trading loss we had suffered the previous financial year through the loss of the magazine revenues, the decision had also been taken to close the general printing and book publishing departments. The Westmorland Gazette was a division of Westminster Press, not an independent company. Westminster Press was in turn owned by Pearsons whose main interest was newspaper printing and publishing with businesses in various parts of the country. Pearsons were also owners of Penguin Books who had taken over another London book publisher, Michael Joseph.

Relinquishing the printing of the magazines had seriously affected our trading performance. General printing was something Westminster Press had become involved with through the acquisition of newspapers which also ran general printing departments. The company had been happy to continue with them so long as there was an acceptable return on the investment. Over recent years, due to poor returns, several of the general printing departments in various parts of the country had closed or been sold off. I began to worry if this was why there was no mention of who the new manager was to be. It was Thursday, Gazette printing day. As the press was running I checked the situations vacant pages - still no advertisement. If the decision had been taken to close the departments, the staff had a right to know. I would go to see Ron Orr, the managing director, the next morning to find out what was happening. After attending to the usual Friday morning routine, not wanting to embarrass Harry Firth, I checked that he was in his office, called into the accounts department on another matter then went down to the MD's office. When I entered Harry sitting there talking to the MD. This was embarrassing - it wasn't something I wanted to raise with him present. If the decision had been taken not to replace him because the two departments he had managed were closing, probably they didn't want Harry to feel he was responsible for about 35 staff losing their jobs. Maybe the MD would wear two caps until the end of the financial year before announcing the closure? Those were my thoughts prior to walking in and seeing Harry there with the MD. 'Good Morning Ron.' There was nothing else for it. I couldn't think of anything else to say. I looked at Harry and apologised saying I thought he was in his office. Now, out with it. 'Still no advert in the Gazette for Harry's replacement? Has it been advertised elsewhere?' 'No,' Ron replied. 'Have a seat - we were just talking about it. Harry thinks you should take it.' I was surprised, it had never crossed my mind that I should succeed Harry. I was happy as I was as the works manager. After some discussion, it became obvious that, due to the considerable financial loss the previous year, this was an opportunity to trim the wage bill. General manager was a more involved proposition than works manager. As works manager I was involved with keeping costs down but not responsible for sales, forecasts, customer liaison etc. I needed time to consider and asked for the weekend to think it over. Taking over as manager when we had made a substantial loss the previous year needed a lot of thought. If we were unable to achieve a reasonable return on the investment there was no doubt the departments would cease to exist. The revenue earned from producing the magazines had been approximately 30 per cent of turnover. It was a lot to lose and replacing it would not be easy. I did not want to be the man in charge if around 35 people were to lose their jobs. Many had been employed at the Gazette all their working lives.

What has all his got to do with Wainwright you are probably wondering? I think it is relevant to later events which resulted in AW being persuaded to do interviews for television, radio, newspapers, magazines and eventually a series of television programmes on the Lake District, the Yorkshire Dales and the Highlands of Scotland before finally agreeing to be interviewed for *Desert Island Discs*.

Monday morning, back in the office, and I had still not decided. I was no nearer a decision than I had been when I left on the previous Friday. There were several good reasons for carrying on as I was as works manager. Why put my head on the block, so to speak? Surely the job would be more suited to someone experienced in sales and marketing? To this day I cannot remember what prompted me but later in the day I agreed to accept the job for a period of two years while also continuing with my responsibilities as works manager on the newspaper side. If I was unable to return the general printing to a profit situation during that time I would stand down in favour of whoever else might be appointed.

A short while later Harry Firth said I should go with him when he next went to see Mr Wainwright and he would introduce me. Friday morning, at about 10.30am, we arrived at a detached property at the top end of Kendal Green, just off Windermere Road, no more than a mile from the office. As we approached, Harry indicated that after being introduced it would be best if I did not sit down until invited. From the little I had heard about this Wainwright chap I thought it just as likely I would be thrown out. Nevertheless, in we went and I was introduced to a large, white-haired, softly-spoken gentleman, badly in need of a haircut and smoking a pipe. I would estimate his height as being at least six feet two inches and his weight around 16 stone. Mrs Wainwright, who I did not meet until the following week, was no more than five feet and I would say seven stones at the very most. After he and Harry Firth had dealt with a few letters which had arrived for him c/o The Westmorland Gazette, I was asked by AW: 'Do you do much walking?' I don't suppose that he was impressed with my reply: 'No, I have four children and quite a big garden. Also, I am still doing alterations and improvements to our house.' It did not occur to me that I could have gained some credibility if I had explained that all my hill climbing experience had been in the Guangdong province of China and Korea as an infantryman during the days of National Service, carrying a rifle, ammunition, hand grenades and two inch mortar bombs in temperatures varying between 30 below to approximately 90 degrees Fahrenheit, often while being shot at or shelled. As a result it was not something I had ever considered doing for pleasure.

Shortly afterwards it was back to the office and down to the business of familiarising myself with the manager's responsibilities. There was a lot to absorb over the next two weeks. At that stage I had not the slightest indication of how important Wainwright and his books were to be to the business in the future.

Even before Harry eventually retired I was under no illusion that, apart from the normal day-to-day running of the business, it was vital some way of replacing the revenue lost through relinquishing the magazine printing contract was found. I had fully expected that someone from higher up in the Westminster Press hierarchy would have contacted me with advice on the best way to improve the trading position overall - but it never happened. All the obvious solutions went through my mind such as increased advertising, employing extra sales representatives, opening branch offices in other districts and so on. One distinct advantage over other local printers was that, as part of The Westmorland Gazette, provided there was space to spare, advertising the facilities of our printing and publishing departments was free, but that in itself wasn't anywhere near enough. If we employed more sales representatives they would need offices, cars, telephones, salaries, pension fund contributions and so on. That route would increase costs at a time when it was crucial they were curtailed and there was no guarantee of improvement even in the longer term. Opening branch offices was also ruled out because that too would mean increased costs without any guarantee of a return. Increasing prices was something which I thought would work up to a point but was just as likely to lose the customers we already had and was not seriously considered. Another disadvantage was the advances in technology being introduced within the industry meaning that some companies could operate with fewer staff. As a result, equipment which was discarded as old technology could be bought for next to nothing and small businesses with very little in the way of overheads were springing up. We ourselves had invested fairly heavily in the new technology but the last resort would have been redundancies. We had good employees, many of whom had been with us for very many years.

No, we needed something to improve our situation in the next year or two. Ideally, some way of increasing revenue without increasing costs. Perhaps the job would have been more suited to a magician.

Time spent in the office outside the usual working hours examining financial records failed to give me a definite lead, but I began to realise that the book publishing side of the business was not exposed to the same competition as the actual general printing. If we could expand book publishing without increasing costs, then we already had the capacity in all production departments necessary to produce more books provided we could sell more. Book sales representatives (we didn't have any at that stage) could be employed on a commission-only basis enabling us to hold our costs through not having to provide offices, cars etc. The more I thought about this approach the more confident I felt about the possibilities. Also taking shape in the deliberations was an indication that the Wainwright books sales could be improved if he could be persuaded to cooperate with regard to doing interviews and publicity in general.

During the last few weeks I had been seeing AW on Monday afternoons and Friday mornings and it had become evident that he was a very private sort of chap and would probably not be interested in disclosing his identity. Something had occurred a few days earlier which confirmed that this fellow Wainwright was more than just an author. His *Pictorial Guide Books to the*

Lakeland Fells had, without him having any indication, earned him cult status in the fell walking fraternity.

During a telephone conversation about the contents of one of the *Guide Books*, the caller realised that I regularly met AW. He was absolutely thrilled that he was speaking to someone who actually knew Wainwright. Like several others I was to come into contact with in the coming months, he had heard or read somewhere that Wainwright was just a pen-name or nom-de-plume for a Gazette journalist and that no such individual existed.

A short time later, I received a telephone call from a customer who had bought one of the *Guide Books* in London and he rang to say it was faulty. One section was duplicated and another section missing. I said we would have a replacement in the post within the next day or two together with a stamped addressed envelope which he could use to return the title page of the faulty book to us. This was standard practice if a book was faulty. A few days later he telephoned again. He had received the replacement book and went on to say how impressed he was at such a quick response. I said if ever he was in Kendal he could call in and I would show him the books being printed in the machine room and bound in the bindery before going into the bookstore ready for despatch. I explained we were easy to find in the town centre, next to Marks and Spencer. Next morning, at about 11.30am, a telephone call from the reception area in our shop told me this chap was there. He said he couldn't wait until he was due in the Lake District again as that would not be for several months and since he had a few days holiday due he had telephoned his boss the previous evening to arrange the day off. The opportunity to see 'the Wainwrights' being produced was worth a special visit. As promised, he was given a tour of the various production departments before leaving him in the bookstore at around 12.30pm where he could browse at his leisure. Come 5pm Tommy Fellowes, the bookstore man, appeared at the door saying he was wanting to lock up before going home but the chap I taken to the bookstore was still there. This was more than four hours since I had left him and he was sitting on a pallet in the bookstore completely engrossed - another example of the prestige of Wainwright.

I also received a request from a chap in London to buy a Wainwright original drawing if one became available. I explained there was a waiting list and took his details. Eventually, after several months, when a drawing became available I contacted him by telephone with the details and the price. He was very keen saying immediately he would like it. Unfortunately, he wouldn't be able to collect for a few days as he was due to leave for Hong Kong the next morning. I was not prepared to risk sending it by post as the price was several hundred pounds. There was no desperate hurry and I would hold on to it until he returned. Next day, late morning, I received a telephone call from our shop saying there was a chap to see me, something about collecting an original drawing. It was the chap to whom I had spoken the day before who was going to Hong Kong. He had postponed his flight. It turned out he was a director of an international company and said he was only going to sack someone so would give him another week. The same chap eventually bought several more drawings whenever they became available.

It was around this time people started to suggest that I should keep records of my dealings with AW - what we discussed, the date, where we were, why we had gone there, was anyone else with us and so on. What they were suggesting confirmed my thoughts that the solution to our revenue problem lay with the promotion and expansion of the book publishing side of the business, especially 'the Wainwrights', thereby providing extra income for the general printing department. The sales aspect was still to be resolved.

Football and *Coronation Street*

AS TIME progressed more events confirmed the high regard and status which AW was earning from the *Guide Books*. For the following two years or more not a lot was achieved with him agreeing to publicity or doing interviews. Whenever the subject was raised it was soon evident that he was not interested. While not being a patient sort of chap, I realised that it was better not to press him too hard. Otherwise our get-togethers were going quite well. We seemed comfortable in each other's company and I was surprised at some things he confided to me. Usually there was just the two of us, Mrs Wainwright often out or occupied in another part of the house. I am sure it helped that I too was from a working class background having started my working life as an errand boy and cleaner before graduating to an apprenticeship in the printing trade. We had several other things in common - we were both interested in our respective football teams, me from the North East, a Sunderland supporter, and AW a founder member of Blackburn Rovers Supporters' Club. If Blackburn had won on the Saturday, Monday's meeting began with him in a superior attitude but if Sunderland won and Blackburn lost, football was a subject best avoided.

After we had dealt with the post he would usually make a cup of tea or coffee and the conversation developed - if not on football it was often *Coronation Street*, which I knew nothing about. I had not seen a single episode so was unable to contribute. I soon realised it might be useful if I could. His favourite character was Jack Duckworth. I was surprised as Jack was a totally different character to himself: Jack liked his pints of beer, AW never drank anything stronger than a half shandy; Jack was a pigeon fancier, AW preferred cats; Jack liked a bet on the horses; I doubt if AW had ever had a bet in his life. Probably the only thing they had in common was that neither were rarely seen without their anorak.

Since retiring from his position of borough treasurer, Animal Rescue, Cumbria had been AW's main interest. He was the charity's chairman and the royalties from his *Guide Books* were donated towards raising sufficient funds for the charity to buy its own headquarters, preferably with outbuildings and some land for exercising the dogs. A committee of ladies was working hard looking after the animals in care and raising funds through jumble sales and sorting and selling anything donated to the cause from a property based in Barrow-in-Furness. AW also donated money raised from the sales of signed original drawings featured in his *Sketchbooks* and *Lakeland Mountain Drawings*.

At this stage the total raised had reached about £35,000. His target was £75,000, or thereabouts, for the price of a property plus whatever was needed to provide outbuildings and a legacy to ensure stray and abandoned animals in the charity's care could be looked after until suitable homes were found. This information was later to prove valuable in persuading him that he should do interviews etc. Very gradually, progress was being made.

At the same time as I was cultivating AW, the other aspect of improving sales needed a lot of thought. I knew little about book publishing and there was no one within either Westmorland Gazette or Westminster Press I could turn to for advice. We were the only office in the whole of the group involved in book publishing. In addition to Westminster Press, Penguin and Michael Joseph were also part of the Pearson empire but that was another world and anyway it was best to keep them at arms' length in case Pearsons decided the larger organisations were better suited to promoting 'the Wainwrights' - which of course they were but it was not something we would suggest.

By chance, about this time someone called into the office to see me about one of our retail outlets in Scotland - he proved to be just the man I needed to give me advice on book sales. He was self-employed, covered the North of England and Scotland, with a wide knowledge of the trade and had many contacts from one end of the country to the other. This was Derek Walker and, through his advice and assistance, I was able to recruit seven representatives to cover England, Scotland, Wales and parts of Ireland, all on a commission-only basis. Things were beginning to fall into place but there was a long way to go before we could reach the goal of raising revenue at least back to the level it had been when we were also magazine printers. The visits to see AW were also being used to keep him informed as to what we were achieving with regard to increased production and our attempts to improve sales in the hope that he might one day volunteer to help in one way or another. I was surprised how well we got on. There was no need to treat him as some sort of celebrity even though, to my mind, what he had achieved in his books put him almost in the 'genius' category. Who else would have thought of beginning such a detailed, time-consuming task of gathering all the necessary information? Even after finding his way to the many locations he needed to visit, more often than not using public transport, he then had to sit down and begin to record what he was seeing as he wished it to appear on paper. Not only was it a matter of writing the text, there were also the maps, the diagrams and the illustrations. And it was not just one book, there are 12 *Guide Books* and then another 38 volumes published by The Westmorland Gazette, all but a few of which were from his own hand rather than typeset. As recently as a few weeks ago I came into contact with someone who, although familiar with the books, found it hard to understand how he managed it all. Conversations with several other people who I will refer to as 'Wainwright enthusiasts' were gradually confirming my belief that the potential was there if only he would agree to publicity.

Copyright

It was around this time that another factor needed to be attended to - copyright. For some reason I had taken it for granted that AW was tied by copyright to The Westmorland Gazette. Normally, if such a document had ever been drawn up, it would almost certainly have been filed in the accounts department but no record could be found. Harry Firth was confident that a contract existed but was not able to produce any documentation. In addition to completed stocks we had tens of thousands of pounds worth of Wainwright books in various stages of production so it was imperative that we were copyright owners. There would be plenty of other publishers willing to take 'the Wainwrights' off our hands if they knew he was not tied by copyright. Fortunately, the Westminster Press directors were due for their annual visit. Following the customary tour of the factory, I raised the matter of copyright, pointing out the importance of the books since the recent investment in new technology had increased our depreciation at a time when revenue had fallen through relinquishing the magazine printing contract. Our chairman, the Duke of Atholl, grasped the importance of the situation and asked me to ring him in his office at 1pm the next day when he would confirm the sum we could offer AW. I was only too pleased to comply and received permission to make the offer which he immediately agreed to, calling through to Mrs Wainwright (who was in the kitchen) that they could start looking for a property for Animal Rescue. Never before, or since that day, did I see AW express such emotion. When I mentioned the figure of £40,000 his face simply beamed. There was an instant uplifting of his spirit. An air of satisfaction and contentment soon developed into the subject of beginning the search for a suitable property. What he had been aiming at for several years had suddenly materialised much earlier than he had anticipated.

Only a few weeks previously I had asked him how long he thought he was going to live and pointed out that, at the current rate of raising funds, he would have to last well into his nineties to achieve his goal. He was in his mid-seventies then and still only at about the half-way stage of his target. By now we knew each other well enough for a bit of mild banter if the mood was right. A few minutes later, when I was about to leave, he asked if I could tell him how long it would be before he received the cheque. I was able to say that I would see our accountant the next morning and bring it with me on Friday but - there was a but - I added: 'You will have to agree to publicity, I need to recoup the £40,000.' It was said in jest really but it served the purpose. Only a few days later, when I accompanied him and Mrs Wainwright to view a property, he mentioned publicity and asked if I had anything in particular in mind. I said: 'No, not really, I wanted to discuss it with you before deciding.' There was a sense of achievement all around.

Television

BY NOW I was becoming more and more ambitious about publicity. Although I had not mentioned it to AW, I had started to think the television people would probably be interested in interviewing him. AW was reasonably cooperative but was not confident they would be interested. I had no contacts at the television companies but, for some reason, decided to try BBC North-East, at Newcastle, and yes, they were interested.

A date a few days hence was suggested and the television crew would arrive late morning. Mid-morning a telephone call came from AW. For some reason there had been a change of heart and he had decided against appearing on television. The television crew had already left Newcastle and, being pre-mobile phone days, there was no way for me to get in touch. It looked like it was going to be a wasted journey - but what could I do? I was quite desperate. It had taken a long time to get to this stage and it was all falling apart at the last minute. The only thing I could think of was perhaps they could interview a few people who knew Wainwright and could talk about him. The next hour or so was spent contacting several people who knew him to enquire if they were available and were they prepared to be interviewed for television? Harry Firth was the first call. Yes, he was in but was not sure about an interview. I was able to persuade him to come to the office to discuss it. Geoffrey Berry was next. Geoffrey was secretary of Friends of The Lake District and had met AW many times in that capacity. He was also a keen fell walker. Harry Griffin, another famous author and mountaineer who, like Geoffrey, lived on the outskirts of Kendal, was also available, as was Percy Duff who had been AW's assistant during his days as borough treasurer. The television people, obviously disappointed at not getting AW, were very understanding, and interviewed the stand-ins and screening went ahead.

My next visit to AW produced a surprise, a very pleasant surprise. He was not happy about some of the things that had been said about him and he was prepared to be interviewed himself to put the record straight.

Excellent, but I needed to be sure he would not have second thoughts again if the television people agreed to come a second time. He assured me he would be interviewed and within days appeared on television. It was a success. The television people were pleased. He was regarded as a catch, never having been interviewed before. Various publications carried articles and there was a marked increase in book orders. Together with a larger than usual number of letters as a result of his appearance on television was a parcel. Letters arrived for him at the Gazette on an almost daily basis but it was the first time for a parcel.

My next Friday mid-morning visit followed its usual pattern – after discussing the mail he would make some coffee while I made a few notes. As he got up to make the coffee he enquired what was in the parcel. I replied that I had no idea but it was addressed to him, c/o Westmorland Gazette, Kendal, and handed it over. My visit the following Monday had him standing there, proud as a little boy, with a new jumper on. 'Look,' he said, 'the parcel.' Two elderly ladies (I seem to remember they were sisters from Gateshead) had seen him on television wearing a jumper with a large hole in the front. A note enclosed said they had had to guess his size but he looked a big man and they hoped the jumpers (they had each knitted one) fitted and that he wouldn't be offended. They need not have worried, he was not offended in any way. In fact he was very pleased and wrote a short thank you note.

Although by this time he accepted that publicity was beneficial and had a marked effect on sales of his books, when the opportunity arose to be interviewed for *Desert Island Discs* he was not at all interested. I had received a telephone call from a Derek Drescher, of BBC Radio, saying that he was responsible for arranging the interviews for the programme and they would like Mr Wainwright to be interviewed by Roy Plomley. For those readers of lesser years, Roy Plomley was the man who was associated with *Desert Island Discs* in those days. He had devised and presented the programme for many years and had become a household name. Most would have regarded it as an honour to be invited but not AW. After discussing it with him I reluctantly had to ring Derek back with the refusal but said I would contact him if I could persuade AW to change his mind. He did of course change his mind but not for a few years. After Roy Plomley had passed away Michael Parkinson took over. I thought there was a possibility here that AW might agree. Parkinson was the type AW would like. He seemed to be a pleasant, straightforward sort but no, he wasn't a Parkinson fan. He did, of course, eventually agree to be interviewed but not until a few weeks after Michael Parkinson had been succeeded by Sue Lawley. More of this later in the book.

In the meantime he was hard work when the question of interviews or any kind of publicity arose. We did not always agree. We did not have to. Publicity was a good example, but I had a job to do and it was vital to the business that we increase book sales. On more than one occasion I found it necessary to point out to him that I was employed by The Westmorland Gazette. They paid my wages and I was in the Westminster Press Pension Fund. Because he was paid royalties he automatically benefitted from any improvement or increase in sales. At one time I was so frustrated trying to make headway with future publicity that I said my time was better spent in the office and had a driver deliver his mail for about six weeks. Perhaps it was because I was prepared to disagree with him rather than simply be someone he could dominate, that we got on so well. There was no doubt, probably from his authority as borough treasurer, he was used to getting his own way.

As time went on my wife, Bernice, and I regularly accompanied AW and Mrs Wainwright on outings or for meals. AW enjoyed his food. Good, bad or indifferent he enjoyed food. His favourites were fish and chips, ice cream and hot custard. I realised, after knowing him for two or three years, that the best time to seek his cooperation was as he finished a meal. Sometimes it was as he put his knife and fork down and lit his pipe. Better still, if we were having coffee, after he had lit his pipe and had taken his first sip, he was then at his most vulnerable. He would sit back and his eyes glazed over. That, I learned, was the time to strike. If that is considered unfair or ungrateful, I admit I am guilty. I used the ploy on several occasions and it worked a treat. Occasionally we were invited to his home at Kendal Green for supper and, on occasions, if they were passing, he and Mrs Wainwright would visit. In winter time he would always sit at the end of the settee which was immediately opposite our open fire. It was not unknown for him to fall asleep.

By the end of 1983, with a steady increase in sales and close control of costs, the general printing department was now back in a profit situation. Not sufficient to sit back. Not even a reasonable return on the investment but at least our efforts were beginning to show results. Interest in AW and his books was growing - in book sales and requests for interviews. If I could generate more publicity there was an increase in sales which was beneficial to both AW and the Gazette.

By this time I had started to keep a list of people wanting to acquire original drawings for, or a copy of, his limited edition of *Westmorland Heritage* which was published in 1975 to officially mark the end of Westmorland as a county. On publication it was sold for £11.50, including post and packaging, but had sold out in three weeks. A copy in mint condition is currently worth several hundred pounds and recently an original drawing for the book was sold for £1,000. By 2008 the asking price for a single copy, unused and in good condition, had reached £65. Later the printing plates used for producing *Westmorland Heritage*, together with the corresponding printed sheets, were mounted and framed. They became known as the Wainwright Westmorland Heritage Plaques and eventually sold out completely. Shortly after they were introduced one was resold for £500. The first day they were on sale in The Westmorland Gazette shop one lady bought a selection of ten of the Langdale Pikes.

Over the next few years AW diaries were something else we introduced and were very successful, with colour photographs supplied by various local Wainwright enthusiasts - several years a reprint was required to meet the demand.

As his popularity grew the demand for original drawings also grew. This sparked the idea of reproducing selected drawings from his *Lakeland Sketchbooks* or *Mountain Drawings* with the name or caption of the subject printed underneath and AW actually signing each one individually. Prices of original drawings had risen to a level which was unaffordable for many people and there were not sufficient becoming available so this was possibly a way of satisfying demand and, at the same time, earning more, much-needed income. Signed prints could be available at a fraction of the price being asked for original drawings. Originally 20 different Lakeland subjects were reproduced and a further four later. AW, prolific as ever with the pen, signed them at the rate of around 1,000 per week. Although they were printed in lots of 2,000 of each subject, I took only 500 for signing, hoping he might be able to complete signing within a fortnight or so. Imagine my surprise when, on my next visit a few days later, they were ready.

The Lakeland selection was followed by 20 from the *Dales Sketchbooks*, 20 from *Kendal in the 19th Century* and, finally, a selection from *Ribble Sketchbook*. In total, he signed more than 40,000.

The issue of his reluctance to be involved with publicity persisted. He wasn't getting any younger and I was running out of ideas. As I have already stated I had no experience of sales or marketing. We needed somehow to promote him to a wider audience than the readership of The Westmorland Gazette and BBC North-East. Advertising in the national press was prohibitive.

For some time Michael Joseph, a subsidiary of Penguin Books, which in turn was owned by Pearsons, the Westminster Press owners, was showing a keen interest in the Wainwright titles but, as I have already said, I was wary of them becoming involved because the possibility of them being preferred by Pearsons as publishers over The Westmorland Gazette would result in all the effort put in over the past two or three years being lost. If the Wainwright books went then that would be the end of our general printing department and approximately 35 jobs. Securing the copyright when we did had been a wise investment and the influence of the Duke of Atholl, the chairman of our Board of Directors, had been to our advantage.

But, looking at the situation realistically, AW was now in his late seventies. He appeared to be in good health but his eyesight was beginning to fail. Michael Joseph had been considering a 'coffee table' type publication. If we agreed to them coming to some agreement with AW for two or three full-colour, glossy books they would not necessarily be competing with us for sales. It was a different type of product and may even be complementary to our Wainwright titles. The publicity they would generate, with the expertise of a professional sales and marketing team, would be far and away above anything we could contemplate and there was a fair chance it would be to our advantage. Yes, the more I thought about it the more it made sense. Ron Orr, our managing director, was not happy with the idea but, when he had time to consider the wider aspects, agreed. Initially we give permission for three titles.

AW welcomed our decision and we gave Michael Joseph the go ahead. Their first title was published jointly with the BBC and accompanied by a series of six half-hour television programmes based on the *Lakeland Guide Books*, exactly what I had been striving for. The first was to be screened in less than two months' time which, in itself, created another problem. After his interview on BBC North-East there had been a considerable increase in sales and that was after only a short interview screened by one region. The six half-hour programmes were to be screened nationwide and there would obviously be a spin-off for sales of the *Guide Books*. Could we produce enough books in two months to meet the anticipated demand? Also, what was the anticipated demand? There was no way of knowing but it would almost certainly be more than we could produce in two months. Extra paper and ink stocks were ordered and, although printing was not a problem, binding sufficient stocks to meet the anticipated increase in demand was much more difficult. The books were all hand bound. As they were used on the fells in all kinds of weather they had to be. We only had three actual recognised bookbinders. Bookbinding assistants could carry out the folding, collating and stitching operations but the glueing, mulling and casing-in was restricted by Union agreements to time-served bookbinders. The only way to achieve the quantities we envisaged would be required was by overtime. Our three bookbinders were given the opportunity to work 12 hours a day, seven days a week for two months. With their cooperation we achieved our targets.

Other television series followed - on Scotland, Coast to Coast, Pennine Way and the Yorkshire Dales - each of which was accompanied by a full-colour book. In the mid 1980s AW had agreed to meet a young amateur photographer from the Halifax area. He was Julian Halstead and, apart from being a keen fell-walker, Julian impressed AW with his skills as a photographer. He was AW's choice to do the photography for the glossy Yorkshire Dales book. Julian was employed full-time by one of the Yorkshire utility companies. Progress on the book was delayed for many weeks to give Julian sufficient time to do the work but his full-time job, together with the arrival of their first child, made it impossible. Eventually he had to decline the opportunity. If it is any consolation to him his disappointment was shared by AW.

AW presented me with a signed copy of each of the first four published which topped the best sellers list. Spin-off sales of his titles published by The Westmorland Gazette increased from 28,000 in 1982 to 87,000 in 1986 - more than 300 per cent in four years without any increase in staff or promotional costs. The permission given originally to Michael Joseph for three titles was conveniently overlooked.

Book Four, The Southern Fells, had for several years been our best seller. However, that changed when *Coast to Coast Walk* was televised. By the time the first episode was broadcast we had built up a stock of more than 10,000 but, within weeks, had to produce a further few thousand as stocks rapidly dwindled. Both AW and I were very surprised. The Coast to Coast route covers some very exposed areas over the Pennines and the North Yorkshire Moors and is in the region of 190 miles long, from St Bees Head in Cumbria to Robin Hood's Bay on the East Coast. But it had caught the imagination of the walking fraternity and remained our best seller for several years afterwards. Information filtered back that many small businesses along the route were enjoying an increase in trade, especially bed and breakfast establishments

In addition to our general printing and book publishing departments, AW and Animal Rescue also benefitted hugely from the increase in sales. Before he retired as an author he had provided Animal Rescue with a reserve fund of more than half-a-million pounds and had formed a trust to re-direct royalties to other deserving animal charities. AW himself was not allowed to decide where the royalties were donated otherwise they would be subject to tax, hence the trust. For several years he had difficulty convincing the tax authority that he was donating all this money to Animal Rescue. When eventually a local tax inspector was due to call on him he asked me to leave our usual Monday meeting until the Tuesday. On the Tuesday visit, I had forgotten about his meeting with the taxman until he said:

'Don't you want to know what happened with the taxman?' I said: 'Yes, how did you get on?' He replied that he had 'grilled him for half-an-hour'. I got the impression that the taxman had received the same treatment as one or two journalists who were given the dubious honour of being assigned to interview him. AW 'interrogated' them before they interviewed him.

Reporter Richard North was unfortunate enough to be assigned to do The Westmorland Gazette's first interview with AW and the account of his experience, published in the February 27, 1991 edition, gives an indication of why AW had earned such a fearsome reputation. They had never previously met and the following is an extract from his article:

It was every reporter's nightmare - a disastrous two hour interview with a subject who just didn't want to talk. At the end of it I had half a page of notes and a cold sweat down my back. The silent interviewee was writer Alfred Wainwright, the Lake District's most famous author since Wordsworth, whose hand-written Guide Books to the Lakeland Fells *had made him a reluctant celebrity. To make matters worse, The Westmorland Gazette had been publishing Wainwright's books for more than 20 years and this was his first-ever interview with the paper. It had already been given advance billing as the day Wainwright broke his self-imposed silence.*

The story that eventually appeared was notable for the way Wainwright maintained his self-imposed silence. It contained not a single quote - I didn't have any - but was strong on observations of his body language: Wainwright refusing to shake hands, Wainwright smiling to himself behind his pipe, and so on. The headline told the whole story, as do all the best headlines. It ran: It's game to Wainwright - he's given nowt away. *His wife told me later that Wainwright rather liked the way he came across as an obstinate old devil with a kind-hearted streak.*

Wainwright's death in January, 1991, at the age of 84, ended an association with The Westmorland Gazette which began in 1963. The first of his unique mountain guides, crammed full of superbly executed drawings, maps, route descriptions and personal asides, was produced by Kendal printers Bateman and Hewitson in 1954. The Gazette became involved when the newspaper's general printing department took over Bateman and Hewitson, and the job of dealing with Wainwright - already a notoriously prickly character - was inherited by printing manager Harry Firth.

Wainwright was a prolific author and produced 50 books in association with the Gazette. Late in life he achieved national recognition with appearances on television and Radio 4's Desert Island Discs, and when his eyesight failed he teamed up with publishers Michael Joseph for a series of best-selling coffee table books.

Wainwright was a one-off. The effort he put into his books was extraordinary, both on the fells and at his writing desk. He would deliver his books to the Gazette's printing department page by page. They contained not a single letter of printer's type, and Wainwright ensured that each line was fully justified, coming to an end with a full word.

Sales of his Gazette-produced books passed the million mark in 1985 and have shown no signs of slowing down. But Wainwright reaped no personal benefit from his books, preferring instead to donate his profits - estimated over the years at £500,000 - to his favourite animal charity.

Westmorland Gazette book publishing manager Andrew Nichol, who dealt with Wainwright for the past nine years, recalls him with a mixture of affection and frustration. 'The Wainwright factor, as I often referred to the connection between The Westmorland Gazette and Wainwright, was never really developed to its true commercial potential,' he says. 'He was our biggest asset, both to the general printing and book publishing departments.' He recalls how Wainwright was finally persuaded to appear on Desert Island Discs after *two years of saying no, with the promise of a slap-up meal at Harry Ramsden's fish and chip restaurant near Bradford. And it was Andrew Nichol who had the task of buying Wainwright's own choice of retirement present from The Westmorland Gazette - four Cornetto ice creams, which he instructed his wife to put in the fridge and refused to share with anybody.*

When it was a case of money for Animal Rescue there was never a moment's hesitation. When it came to spending for himself that was another matter, apart from tobacco and ice cream. During one visit, Mrs Wainwright came to me with one of his shirts saying: 'Look Andrew, AW wants me to turn the collar but it has already been turned. Will you tell him he needs a new one?' It was in tatters but he would not give her the money for a new one. On another occasion when we were going to Manchester he appeared in a pair of bright green trousers. I could not believe he would go out in them – they were really only suitable for gardening! After a few minutes he asked what I thought of them. 'They were only £13 in Milnthorpe market,' he said. He must have deduced something from my reply. I never saw them again.

It was mid 1980s when a property came up for sale just a short distance down the road from his house. He kept trying to persuade me to consider selling my own house and purchasing it but, although we got on well, I thought three mile or thereabouts was near enough. On occasions when Mrs Wainwright went away for a few days visiting her daughters from her first marriage, I made a point of going most mornings to see if he was comfortable, particularly in winter times, and offered to light the coal fire and fill the coal scuttle. But he was always content with one bar of the electric fire.

Reports that he and Peter, his son from his first marriage, did not get on were untrue. More often than not when I went at weekends when Mrs Wainwright was away, Peter would arrive with a packet of AW's favourite boiled sweets. I could never understand the statement he made in his book *Ex-Fellwanderer* that he was not going to leave anything for the next generation. That was AW's way of referring to his only son who visited him on a regular basis and always brought him a packet of sweets.

The subject of AW's first marriage was something he refused to discuss for many years and dealt with only briefly in *Ex-Fellwanderer*. Peter's wife, Doreen, has fond memories of her mother-in-law Ruth, describing her as a well read, much travelled lady who enjoyed cooking and pastry baking, renowned especially for her steak and kidney pies, custard tarts and lemon meringues, produced for family gatherings. Despite having to obtain most of her clothes from charity shops due to AW's refusal to hand over a reasonable housekeeping allowance, she describes Ruth as being very smart. Eventually, only a few weeks before AW was to retire, due to his indifference to their marriage she walked out and, with Peter, found accommodation in Windermere where she became popular and lived happily. Doreen also remembers that, before leaving, Ruth left a list of matters AW would need to attend to and a well-stocked panty. It was only when confronted with the prospect of the break-up of his marriage that AW relented, offering Ruth a substantial increase in her housekeeping allowance if she would stay, but her mind was made up. AW was never to see her again. Peter, who was born in 1932, became an engineer employed for a number of years in Bahrain on gas pipelines. He married Doreen, a local girl, in 1973 and returned to live in the Lake District. He became a representative in the printing trade. One customer with whom Peter had dealt for a good number of years was not to learn until after Peter's death in September 1998 that he was AW's son.

AW's nephew, Jack Fish, also remembers Ruth with fondness. When he heard that I was considering writing this book, he asked if the following could be included to correct the impression given in *Ex-Fellwanderer* that Ruth was just a humble mill girl.

I was seven years old when I attended the wedding of my uncle, Alfred Wainwright, to Ruth Holden in the Congregational Church in Blackburn. From then on she became Auntie Ruth and was to play a large part in my life. After their son Peter was born and before they moved to Kendal, Ruth always gave Peter a birthday party and, being the eldest of the cousins, I went along to entertain. Auntie Ruth was a fun person. She often arranged picnics and I well remember she took Peter and me on a walk over Pendle Hill, taking with us a little stove, a pan and some water – and at the top of Pendle we boiled eggs.

She loved animals and, just before they moved to Kendal (Alfred had gone ahead to arrange living accommodation) she and Peter came to live with my family for several weeks, bringing with her Peggy the dog, Paddy the cat, a budgie, a tortoise and a white mouse.

After they moved to Kendal we still remained close and I visited many times and Ruth, Peter and I spent memorable holidays together – the Festival of Britain in 1951; a tour by coach across France, through Italy to Naples and across to the Isle of Capri where we met Gracie Fields. On another occasion we went by train across France, Germany and Austria to Vienna. All these trips were arranged by Auntie Ruth on our behalf.

After she had obtained a divorce from AW, I visited her regularly in her new Windermere home, as did my brother Alan, his wife and their two boys. Each time she took us to a new place to visit (mainly with a garden attached as she had an interest in plants) and to enjoy afternoon tea.

Auntie Ruth was very intelligent, well read and a well travelled person.

In later years she became crippled with arthritis and, in time, moved to a nursing home in Sedbergh. She died in 1985 and I shall always remember her as a special person.

It was AW's wish that, on his death, the book sales would cease and the original drawings would be destroyed. To my mind unthinkable, but to AW the drawings were nothing out of the ordinary. He stuck to his word about not leaving anything to the next generation, not even an original drawing. When the Westmorland Heritage Plaques were put on sale it was left to The Westmorland Gazette to make a present of one to Peter who, although not quite as tall as his father, was much the same build. On his arrival at the office to select a plaque I left him with the sample selection book, sitting with his back to the doorway while I attended to something else in the works. On returning, as he came into view it was as if it was his father with his back to me - the build was the same, the posture was the same, even having the toes of his left foot curled around the front, left side leg of the chair. The likeness was uncanny and brought back happy memories.

At the same time as I was trying to persuade AW to appear on television I occasionally mentioned that any correspondence connected with his works, particularly anything of an official nature, should be preserved for future reference. I was convinced that his life and achievements would be of interest to local historians but he thought it unlikely. Eventually I was able to convince Mrs Wainwright to store anything at all in their cellar. Filing or recording was not important so long as it was saved. During a reorganisation at The Westmorland Gazette I moved into a smaller office at the other side of the building.

It meant having a thorough clearout including returning two manuscripts he had produced, one for *Fellwalking with a Camera* and one for *Ex-Fellwanderer*, together with some original artwork and the artwork he had produced for a certificate planned to be awarded to those who had completed the Three Peaks Walk. He said he did not want them and again, when I suggested they be stored in his cellar, he insisted there was no space to spare and said: 'You have them if you want them.' I gratefully accepted and several years ago passed them on to my grandchildren for their future benefit.

At about the same time I said that, if he agreed to appear on television, as an investment I would buy a copy of everything he had had published by the Gazette and would want him to sign each copy. When the day actually arrived and he was doing the signing on the table in his living room I started thinking about how long it would have taken him to do a typical drawing such as those in the *Sketchbooks* or *Mountain Drawings*. My first estimate was probably one to two days per drawing. Then I remembered that he did not start the *Lakeland Guide Books* until the mid fifties, then there was *Fellwanderer*, *Pennine Way Companion*, *Limestone Country*, *Howgill Fells*, *Coast to Coast Walk*, *Outlying Fells* etc. Also all the drawings for the *Sketchbooks* and *Mountain Drawings*. Then take into account the time spent doing the reconnaissance work for the *Guide Books*, travelling by bus while working full time until retirement in 1967 followed by many years of voluntary work at Kendal Museum. Also, even Wainwright had to eat and sleep. When he had finished the signing I asked: 'How long did it take you to do a drawing?' The answer was typical Wainwright: 'Oh, it varied quite a lot, there was a lot more work in some than others. Some I would do in about an hour-and-a-half, others took up to two hours.' Without wishing to overdo the adulation, I have no hesitation in using the word 'incredible'.

With a pen in his hand, AW was a genius. With a tool of any description he was hopeless. Arriving for a visit when Mrs Wainwright was away, as he opened the door he said: 'I am in trouble.' I replied: 'Why, what have you been up to?' and followed him into the kitchen. The plug, or stopper, had separated from the chain in the kitchen sink. I went to the car for a pair of pliers, put it back on and nipped the split link up again. It only took a minute or two and I went back into the living room and said it was mended. He was amazed I had done it so quickly. I said: 'It was the split link that had opened up and it just needed nipping up again,' but I doubt if he even knew what a split link was. Recently, the late Percy Duff (who had served as AW's deputy during his tenure as borough treasurer) and I were reminiscing about such occasions. We had both served in the Army, Percy during the war and myself as a National Serviceman after the war, and agreed it was probably a good thing that AW was never 'called up'. The thought of AW with a lethal weapon was a frightening proposition. The rest of the Army was safer with AW at home with a pen.

His office, workroom and studio was a spare bedroom. Apart from a table and chair that he used, there was only one other chair, a shelf or two and that was about it. He spent hours there, coming downstairs only at mealtimes or in the evening when he had finished for the day. There was no telephone extension simply because he would not answer the telephone. If you needed to get in touch, and Mrs Wainwright was not at home, you had to visit. In all the time I was involved with him I doubt if he used the telephone more than a dozen times. He was perfectly happy in his studio - the only regular visitor being

AW and Peter in earlier days.

Haystacks: from the youth
        hostel an
        Honister Pass.

1. take the A591 to keswick

2. then the B5289 to
   SEATOLLER in BORROWDALE

3. Stop for an ice cream

4. then drive up Honister
   pass to the youth
   hostel on the left.
   You can park in their
   carpark (busy in summer)
   you will need change
   for the ticket machine.

5. the path to Haystacks
   is on the left, just after
   the youth hostel it runs
   straight as a die after
   the initial ascent,
   Due west.

N.B. from the path: on your
left you can see
GREY KNOTTS, BRANDRETH
GREEN + GREAT GABLE, KIRK
FELL.
To your right Dale Head
+ ROBINSON: You will walk
across Fleetwith.   P.T.O.

once on Haystack looking
Towards Lake Buttermere
the ridge to the left of
the lake is HIGH CRAG
HIGH STYLE and the
pointy one is RED PIKE

Looking across ENNERDALE
valley you can see PILLAR

Wainwright's Pictorial
            Guides 6+7

show the fells to the
east + west of Buttermere

AWs directions to Innominate Tarn. Step 3 was essential.

Preparing to abscond when he spotted the camera.

Negotiating: Just holiday snaps, not something for publication.

Negotiations failed. Taking no chances.

AW's idea of posing for a photographs

AW, Betty and Bernice relaxing before dinner at Ballachulish.

Our accommodation at Duirinish

Admiring the Scottish scenery.

AW alone with his thoughts

Unaware of the camera.

AW and me at Little Langdale. Photo: Ken Shepherd

AW trying to avoid someone who had recognised him.

The brock from the Scottish
television series.

Son Peter with his wife, Doreen.

Family gathering at Kendal Green: from the left, brother-in-law Bill, sister Alice, first wife Ruth, other sister Annie and nephew Jack Fish.

AW's silver wedding anniversary, with one important face missing ... out fell walking.

Totty, his favourite cat. They had rescued Totty when she was only a few days old and could hardly walk, hence the name. Out of their nine cats Totty was the only one to venture into his workroom. She would jump onto the table and sit on whatever he was doing. He would put his pen down, light his pipe and say she was telling him it was time to have a rest.

I must have been visiting him for three to four years before I was ever invited to see him upstairs. He was not feeling too well and preferred to stay in his workroom. The next hour or so was an experience I found difficult to understand and find it even more difficult to describe. As I have already said, the room was sparsely furnished with only two old kitchen chairs and a table and no more than about ten feet by eight, but on entering I sensed the atmosphere was quite different to the rest of the house. The nearest I can get would be to say it was a reverence or a serenity normally only found in a place of worship. I cannot ask anyone else for their opinion because I do not know anyone else who was invited into the room. I had the idea of photographing his office with a view to offering to replicate it in Kendal Museum for posterity but when he passed away Mrs Wainwright had already changed it before I had the opportunity to make the suggestion.

Brantwood

I HAD often felt that AW should be commemorated in some way and was pleased to hear that he had received a visitor who was interested in establishing a Wainwright exhibition. It was to be on a permanent basis and situated at Brantwood, near Coniston, well known as the former home of the poet and author John Ruskin. The proposer was Bruce Hanson, at that time the curator at Brantwood, and AW, after some thought, agreed to the idea and would supply several items for display including the old Harris Tweed jacket featured in a cartoon in one of the *Guide Books*, his old typewriter, a redundant pipe and ashtray and so on. Prior to the opening, Bruce invited AW to visit Brantwood to seek his approval on various items and we had lunch with Bruce in the Brantwood Cafeteria. Shortly after leaving, AW commented on how much he had enjoyed the sherry trifle. I agreed with him. It was absolutely superb. At a date nearer to the opening Bruce requested AW to make a second visit but AW, typically, did not want to go back. Bruce eventually sought my advice on how we might persuade him. After some thought I mentioned that there may be a chance if he promised another sherry trifle as AW had commented how good the first one was. Bruce said the lady who had made the trifle no longer worked there but was confident she would make another, if asked. I agreed to go even if AW would not. The next step was to try to persuade AW. My next visit followed the usual practice - deal with the mail, discuss this and that, avoid mentioning football if Blackburn had lost their last match and so on. As I was about to leave I mentioned that I would have to miss my next visit because I was going to Brantwood. As Bruce had been unable to persuade him to go, I told AW he had asked me if I could help, adding that he had offered to put on another trifle. Can you guess who was in the front passenger seat when I went back? It took all of two minutes in the exhibition for AW to advise Bruce and then it was down to the more important aspect of our visit. Yes, it was trifle time and, because it was such a pleasant, warm day, we decided to eat on the terrace rather than in the cafeteria. Out came the bowl of trifle and Bruce served three large portions. It really was excellent and I just about managed to finish mine, the helping was so generous. One helping was also sufficient for Bruce but AW thought he might manage a second. We then talked about various aspects of the exhibition and AW agreed to return for a pre-opening appearance for Press photographers. I was just about to stand up ready to leave when AW kindly offered to finish what was left so they could wash the bowl. Long before we left he had been recognised and a small crowd had gathered but kept a discreet distance. Having been well fed he was in a good mood and signed a few autographs. When the day arrived for his appearance for the photographers I was envisaging a last minute change of heart but, apart from being a little quiet on the way, there was no problem. We arrived via the rear entrance to Brantwood and walked down to the exhibition room. Due to his poor eyesight I had to tell him how many steps etc. and after seeing him inside said I would come back in a quarter-of-an-hour. There were about 15 photographers and they were patient and considerate. Due to the small area only two or three could work at any one time.

Following the death of AW, Mrs Wainwright had the contents of the Brantwood exhibition transferred to Kendal Museum which she thought was a more appropriate venue considering the amount of time AW had spent there doing voluntary work after his retirement.

Desert Island Discs

A TELEPHONE call from Derek Drescher, of BBC Radio, explaining that he was responsible for arranging the subjects chosen to be interviewed by Roy Plomley for *Desert Island Discs* and they would like to interview Mr Wainwright, came unexpectedly. I replied that I would pass the message on when

I next visited Mr Wainwright but, because he usually avoided publicity, I was not very hopeful. The response from AW was as predicted and reluctantly I had to return Derek's call with a promise that if I could persuade AW to change his mind I would get back in touch. Derek offered to telephone him direct but I had to explain we were not allowed to disclose his telephone number. On several occasions I tried to persuade AW that it was a golden opportunity but he was not interested. About three years after first being invited onto the programme he said something mildly complimentary about Sue Lawley, who had recently succeeded Michael Parkinson as presenter. I wondered if it was worth raising the subject again as I was sure the sales of his books would increase after such nationwide publicity. Apart from the prestige I thought *Desert Island Discs* would reach a different audience to the television programmes which were broadcast in the evenings. *Desert Island Discs* was transmitted during the morning. I decided that I should first check the invitation still stood. On ringing the number previously given to me by Derek Drescher I was told that Roy Plomley had died and Derek had moved onto something else. The job was now being done temporarily by Gillian Hush. I was put through to Gillian who said they were still interested, in fact when Sue had taken over they had discussed Wainwright but there was a note on his file that he was not interested. I explained that something AW had said a day or two earlier had made me hopeful there was a change of heart but I would have to think how to raise the subject again because, if he refused, another few years could be lost. There was some hard studying to do. I remembered that recently, probably two months or so previously, he had commented he had never been on the M62. I replied that he should consider himself lucky as I had been on the M62 several times and, for one reason or another, always seemed to run into a hold-up. The fact that he had never been on the M62 was not a lot to go on. I needed something more than that. Linking the M62 with being interviewed for *Desert Island Discs* needed some imagination. The next day I decided not to get involved with any work problems so as to devote most of the day to considering the AW and *Desert Island Discs* conundrum. I still felt part of the solution would involve the M62 and probably a fish and chip meal. Then, out of the blue, the telephone rang. It was Gillian. Was there any chance of getting AW? They were having a problem with someone who was playing hard to get and they would much prefer AW. I thought to myself AW was also playing hard to get but the fact that Gillian had rung at the very time the subject was uppermost in my mind made me think that we should 'go in at the deep end' and hope for the best. 'Leave it with me Gillian. I will go straight to see him. I will ring you back if there is any progress but do not be surprised if you never hear from me again.' AW answered the door with the words: 'Hello, I wasn't expecting you today.' I replied: 'I've been thinking, you said a few weeks ago that you had never been on the M62. If you agreed to do *Desert Island Discs* we could go to Manchester for the interview, go along the M62 to Bradford, turn off at Bradford, go to Harry Ramsden's at Guiseley for fish and chips, come back through the Dales and stop somewhere for an ice cream.' His reply absolutely staggered me. 'Yes, alright.' After all that time it was as simple as that.

I got out quickly in case he changed his mind, rang Gillian with the news and explained what I had promised. Momentarily I was in for a shock. Gillian said: 'All the interviews are done in London.' My heart sank. London? He will never agree to go to London. He hated going to London. Then Gillian said: "I'll ring Sue, her husband is our manager and she has never seen his office. She will welcome the opportunity to come to Manchester.' Relief. Next thing, warn Alan Rangeley, our production manager, that extra supplies of paper would be needed and to re-introduce the 12-hour days, seven days a week in the bookbinding department. A few days later Gillian travelled to Kendal to discuss with AW his selection of records and various other matters prior to the actual recording and confirmed that Sue Lawley was quite happy to travel to Manchester to do the interview. One of the records he chose was not known to the BBC. Fortunately he still had his copy in the cabinet. Typical AW - he said it was about the sixth one along from the left and he was right. Gillian had to borrow it to use for the broadcast.

On the day we were due in Manchester for the recording it was a relief to see him standing outside waiting for me. It had been something of a worry since he had changed his mind at the last minute on the day of his first television interview. Mrs Wainwright was not in favour of him doing *Desert Island Discs* so it was just AW and me. On arrival at the studios we spent the first 15 minutes or so in casual conversation before Sue Lawley explained what the procedure was before recording began and said it would not begin until he felt ready. He said he would like to visit the 'little boys' room' and while he was away she asked if there was anything he particularly liked to talk about which would help him to relax. I said that he was proud to have been a founder member of Blackburn Rovers Supporters' Club and that would probably be as good as anything. On his return Gillian Hush and I retreated into a room separated from the recording room by a soundproof glass partition and where the sound recordist was at a desk. We could see and hear everything and at the end of the interview Gillian remarked that they had enough material for two programmes. Afterwards we had lunch in the BBC canteen. Since AW and myself were going on to Harry Ramsden's we only had a sandwich. I had heard jokes about the food in BBC canteens without taking them seriously but we were both amazed at how difficult it was to actually swallow the bread. When we got onto the M62 AW asked me what I thought of my sandwiches and I mentioned the difficulty I had in swallowing the bread. He pulled his handkerchief out of his pocket complete with chewed sandwich. He said he had not been able to swallow it either and had to keep pretending to wipe his nose.

We heard later from Gillian that the response from listeners after the broadcast was one of the best ever. One lady who listened to the programme each week as she drove to her office in London wrote to Sue Lawley saying that although she had driven the same route for several years she was so entranced listening to AW she somehow got on the wrong road and lost her way. As I had expected, the demand for books shot up and sales stayed high for several weeks.

By this time I had found that any publicity generated requests for more interviews but had to be careful not to overdo it. If he was asked too often it would almost certainly result in him refusing them all. It was best to wait and say casually that such and such a newspaper, magazine or radio station had been on the telephone and I had promised to get back to them if he agreed. That way it did not feel as if I was putting him under pressure and he sometimes did agree fairly quickly. To one request he agreed immediately adding: 'Tell him it will cost him lunch at the Little Chef.' The interview was conducted in the back of my car on the Little Chef car park, at Ings - after he had had his lunch.

While filming was in progress for the television series based on the *Lakeland Guidebooks* there was no need for me to be there but after several days AW invited me along. The meeting point the next morning was to be at the Black Sail Youth Hostel but, on arrival, it was pouring with rain. Richard Else, the producer for the series, said a room had been reserved at the Wordsworth Hotel, in Grasmere, where we should go for some indoor filming in the form of a question and answer session with Eric Robson, the *Gardeners' Question Time* chairman, who was to talk and interview AW through each of the programmes. After a short while there AW asked for the room to be cleared while he raised something he obviously was not happy with. We spent 15 minutes or so outside before Richard appeared to say we could go back in. When the same thing happened again a short time later I decided my time was better spent at the office and left. It was a matter for Richard. I hoped that whatever the problem was he could resolve it as the television programmes were the answer to my prayers where book sales were concerned. My next visit to Kendal Green took the usual form of dealing with the mail etc. before AW made some coffee. He then asked if I had been wondering what was going on at Grasmere and I replied that after we had been asked to leave the room a second time I had decided to go back to the office. I was serving no purpose there as it was Richard's responsibility. He said he wondered where I had got to and then explained that the question and answer session needed constant revision and he felt that the problems could only be sorted out without the production team looking on.

The Publishers' Association

AW DID agree to do one interview. It was at a time when I had received requests from possibly seven or eight different publications but that number was out of the question. I suggested we offer an interview to the Publishers' Association, a London-based organisation which would circulate the interview to its contributors, which covered almost every publication in the UK and probably some abroad. As I left he said: 'Tell them to send someone with nice legs.' Next morning a telephone call to the Publishers' Association found them happy to agree to send a reporter to which I added his stipulation of sending someone with nice legs. The response was astounding. 'We don't employ females.' At first I thought they were joking but no, they were serious, they did not employ females. I was stumped. What could I do? After a moment's pause I asked if they had any males with nice legs. He promised to do his best. The reporter eventually arrived and, before going to see AW as was the standard practice, I explained he could be difficult on interviews or could be very relaxed. It was just a case of taking things slowly to begin with and advised against asking questions other than those connected with his books or the Lake District in particular. Questions about his private life would almost certainly bring the interview to an immediate end. I thought it prudent not to show him a copy of Richard North's interview. He was not remotely what AW had hoped for when he asked for someone with nice legs. Of stocky build and wearing a long overcoat, even with AW's failing eyesight he would be able to see the difference. Off we went to Kendal Green. He seemed a little nervous. Maybe I had overdone the briefing. I rang the bell. After a minute or so the door began to open very slowly, there was no sound except a slight creaking. AW appeared, looked him up and down and asked: 'Have you got nice legs?' The reporter looked straight ahead at the massive figure in front of him and said nothing. Not a word. AW looked in my direction, shook his head, turned around and walked into the living room followed by the reporter. More than an hour later the reporter reappeared, possibly a little relieved and I am sure quite pleased with how things had gone.

Ordnance Survey

AW WAS a great admirer of Ordnance Survey and readily accepted an invitation for a photographic session with one of its photographers to be held in the Lake District. He loved maps and could spend hours browsing them. On the agreed date we ventured to the chosen spot for the session in front of the camera. Almost an hour was spent with AW in various poses with an Ordnance Survey map in hand. This was probably about two years prior to his death and after his eyesight had deteriorated. It all went very well until the photographer returned to the Ordnance Survey offices in Southampton and developed the photographs. AW was holding the map upside down - fortunately, not on all the photographs. The photographer contacted me at a later date saying: 'Thank you for arranging the session with AW,' and how much his reputation had risen within the company since. The managing director hadn't previously acknowledged him if they met in the building but since he had photographed AW they were on 'nodding terms'.

The One Millionth Book

A UNIQUE opportunity to promote the books arrived when the Gazette order clerk, Mrs Cooke, drew my attention to the fact that we were nearing the point of producing the one millionth Wainwright book. At the current rate of sales it would be only a matter of two or three months ahead. I asked her to monitor the figures closely and to keep me informed. In the meantime I discussed it with AW who, true to form, personally did not want to be involved and preferred something low key. He did, however, agree that we should somehow mark the book so that, after being sold, a publicity campaign could help us locate the book and, with the owner's agreement, would rebind it in leather with gold lettering on the cover to the effect that it was the one millionth Wainwright book produced by The Westmorland Gazette. AW agreed to this and we decided the modification would be his signature below the wording 'Some personal notes in conclusion' which appeared near the end of each of the seven *Lakeland Guide Books*. It was usual for AW to sign things in green but because that would be too easily recognisable with everything else in the book printed in black I suggested, in this instance, his signature should also be in black to ensure his followers had an equal chance of becoming the owner. An extra means of identifying the book was added as a precaution against the possibility of his signature being fraudulently printed in another volume - very difficult but not impossible. The millionth edition was a copy of *Book Six, The North Western Fells*, which went to a retail outlet in the Manchester area. The location was known only to myself, Mrs Cooke and AW. The publicity announcing that the book was now on sale was released and created a tremendous amount of interest. We learned later of quite a few people scouring their local bookshops hoping to recognise something different among copies of *Book Six* on the shelves. Shortly before the book went on sale, a telephone call from the restaurant at the Langdale Timeshare complex offered a free meal for two people with Mr Wainwright as an additional prize if AW agreed, which I thought was very unlikely but promised to put it to him. I was more than surprised when he accepted and this was also publicised. Something like six weeks went by with the book still unsold when one morning I received a telephone call from AW. He wanted to go to Manchester and buy the book himself. I explained the difficulties involved after all the publicity it had attracted but there was no way he would change his mind. We went to Manchester. I refused to go into the shop for the book so he had to go in to buy it himself. On the return journey he confided that he was worried about having a meal with strangers and wished he had not agreed. After further discussion he agreed to the book going back on sale as long as the offer of a meal with the eventual purchasers of the book could be withdrawn, which was easily arranged. Back in Kendal the book was placed in an order from one of our fastest-selling retailers, Chaplin's of Keswick. Two weeks later it was sold but, despite much publicity, has never been found. That particular year there had been a large number of visitors from the Far East and my guess is that it was bought by someone who had returned home before the means of identification was released. In the event of the book being located after I have 'left this world', the additional means of identification has been explained to several friends. For obvious reasons I cannot disclose the additional means in this book. Before you go to bed tonight can I suggest you check your copy of *North Western Fells* and, if it bears the A. Wainwright signature, in black, below the wording 'Some personal notes in conclusion' a few pages from the back of the book, contact me via The Westmorland Gazette for verification through the extra means of identification. Do not let it out of your sight as it will attract interest from quite a few prospective buyers and a lot of attention from the media.

The Proposed Statue

AS THE Westmorland Shopping Centre, in Kendal's Stricklandgate, was nearing completion, the developers offered to provide a life-size, bronze statue of AW within the precinct. As was expected he was not in favour of the idea and for several days would not even venture into Kendal to inspect the proposed site. I was eventually able to persuade him to do so by collecting him and walking the short distance from the Gazette car park to the precinct. It was a fruitless exercise. He was not interested and after returning to his house on Kendal Green made it abundantly clear that he did not want a memorial of any kind. I said I had it in mind that, after his lifetime, we might have an informal 'Wainwright Appreciation Society.' There would be no formal membership and the only activity would be an annual gathering, for all those wishing to attend, on Haystacks, probably on the first Sunday in May. As was customary with AW when he wanted to make something clear, leaning slightly forward, pipe in his right hand pointing towards his 'prey' and speaking in a soft voice, I was to receive three stipulations to be observed after his death. The first was: 'No, I do not want any memorial of any kind.' The second was: 'I do not want anyone writing about me after my death.' He explained he had written *Ex-Fellwanderer* as his autobiography and, as it covered the break-up of his first marriage together with details of his family problems when he was a young lad in Blackburn, there was no need for any additional publications about his life. The third was to the effect, 'he did not want his name used in connection with any commercial enterprise'. Even though his wishes have been widely publicised, the latter two have long since been ignored with the publication of several books preceding this and countless articles in both newspapers and magazines. His name has been used to promote everything from walking boots to mint cake and woolly hats to Wainwright beer which is ironic as, except for the occasional half-shandy with a meal, he was teetotal, refusing even a celebratory glass of sherry at the opening of the Wainwright Exhibition at Brantwood.

Many years later, when a proposal was mooted to develop The Westmorland Gazette site into a shopping area, the council sought suggestions for a name for the walkway leading off from Stricklandgate, through the development past the relocated Gazette offices, to the site of a new Booths supermarket. They selected 'Wainwright's Yard'. I was horrified and those who knew AW will understand my sense of humour when I say I would not have been at all surprised if the telephone had rung and AW was on the line reminding me of his list of things he did not want.

Most recently, another proposal by Kendal Town Council to erect a statue in his 'honour' would have been regarded by him as an affront to his dignity. When the proposal was announced in The Westmorland Gazette, almost every contributor to the newspaper's letters and opinions pages was opposed. The references to statues of Eric Morecambe erected at Morecambe and Laurel and Hardy at Ulverston are in keeping with their professions as entertainers. AW was of a different category. He would never go with the throng and preferred to keep his privacy. He never learned to drive a car, never flew in an aeroplane, never took a foreign holiday, never owned a mobile 'phone and refused to join any clubs or organisations after his retirement. His interests were creative - his *Guidebooks*, the *Sketchbooks*, the *Mountain Drawings* – and he spent many hours at Kendal Museum doing voluntary work. He raised and donated more than half-a-million pounds for Animal Rescue, while at the same time quietly promoting Kendal and the Lake District. I imagine the council considered a statue would be an appropriate posthumous reward for such a famous resistant. However, if his request that there be no memorial of any kind is to be ignored, may I suggest the £70,000 or £80,000 mentioned in connection with the proposed statue be utilised for something more closely allied to his way of thinking. AW was always proud of the fact that his books were produced in Kendal and they provided jobs for at least half-a-dozen local people. He also made an annual bequest of £500 which was awarded to the person who did the most for the benefit of Kendal and its people during the previous year. Would the £70,000 or £80,000 proposed for the statue be better used to provide training or employment for young, local people to give them a start in life? There are a number of people, including myself, who would be prepared to make a donation in his memory to a cause of this kind. I repeat my earlier claim that AW, without doubt, would have regarded a statue as an affront to his dignity.

Channel Four

WE WERE having a more or less routine meeting, nothing much out of the ordinary, when AW casually said: 'I am not doing any more television.' So far as I can recall, that particular day there had been no mention of television and there was nothing due for screening. It took me completely by surprise. Of course, I had hoped there would be more programmes in the future. His eyesight was failing badly but television was an aspect less affected by his disability than writing or producing drawings. Walking while being filmed was more or less out of the question but with four wheel drive vehicles, half-tracks or helicopters transporting him to a particular mountain top or into an accessible valley, broadcasting was still a possibility. He did not enlarge on his statement and I thought it wise to leave it at that, at least for the time being. Two or three weeks later I ventured to ask if it was because of his eyesight but no, not particularly. After a short silence he indicated he was unhappy with something to do with previous programmes and disappointed with the BBC. Again the subject came to an end without me being much wiser. Over the next month I pondered his statement. Did he mean he was not doing any more television full stop or did he mean he would not do any more with the BBC? During my next visit, after the mail had been dealt with and he had made some coffee and was quite relaxed, I said: 'A few weeks ago you said you were not doing any more television because you were not happy with the BBC. Does than mean no more television at all or no more with the BBC?' A short pause and then he said: 'Do you think somebody else would be interested?' I replied that I thought ITV would. He asked if I knew anyone at ITV. I said no but I had once had a pub lunch with Bob Smithies, the newsreader who was based at Lancaster. I could ask Bob to whom I should speak. 'Yes, alright, if you think they will be interested.' Relief. I was optimistic about the outcome. A telephone call to Bob stating a preference for Channel Four, so that we would have countrywide coverage, was made and he said it might take a day or two but he would make some enquiries.

The reply from Bob had encouraging news - Channel Four was interested. He gave me a number to call to make an appointment to meet Rod Caird, a senior executive of Channel Four at the Granada Studios, in Manchester. It was an easy conversation. Within an hour it was agreed in principle that a series of six half-hour programmes based on the *Lakeland Guide Books* could be made. Because of AW's age, and the problem with his eyesight, the producers would limit his involvement to half-a-day for each half-hour programme and would provide whatever means were necessary to get him to wherever he was needed. Our discussion was interrupted several times because one of their camera crews was being held hostage in the Middle East and he was involved by telephone. Only one more thing to discuss: 'Can you give me some indication as to what AW would be paid because, although it would not necessarily be the deciding factor, he would almost certainly ask?' Rod asked if I knew what he was paid by the BBC. I said: 'Yes, but I did not think I should disclose that.' He understood, thought for a moment or two then gave me an 'around about' figure which would need to be ratified by the executive committee. I wished him well with the hostage negotiations and headed back to Kendal. The figure for AW was considerably more than he had been paid by the BBC. I was confident he would be happy with that. However, my surprise at the figure Channel Four would probably pay him was nothing compared to the surprise I was to get when I started to give an account to the Wainwrights of how the meeting had gone. I had not got as far as disclosing the figure AW would have received for the proposed series when Mrs Wainwright joined in the conversation with an ultimatum: 'No more television until we get an increase in royalties.' I was taken aback. The percentage demanded was considerable and unacceptable from The Westmorland Gazette's point of view. AW had never mentioned that he was unhappy with his royalties. There was no point in continuing the conversation. We had many thousands of pounds tied up in slow-selling stock such as the *Lakeland Sketchbooks*, *Lakeland Mountain Drawings*, *The Dales Sketchbooks*, *Scottish Mountain Drawings* and so on. Only the *Guide Books* really justified the capital outlay necessary to tie up large sums of money but we were prepared to take the view that if we were to enjoy the benefits from the *Guide Books* it was reasonable enough that we should continue with the slow-selling lines. For those who are not familiar with the author/publisher arrangement: usually the author is paid a percentage of the retail selling price of the book which, together with the discounts to wholesalers or retailers, leaves the publisher with approximately 50 per cent of the retail selling price. From this remaining 50 per cent the publisher has to pay the printer plus all costs related to storage, packing and delivery, and the publisher's own staffing costs. To agree to the increase would reduce the profit level below that which was necessary to justify the capital outlay to publish. Until that time I had been of the opinion that everyone involved was pleased with how things had improved since 1982. The general printing department was back in profit, Animal Rescue's financial situation had gone from having raised somewhere in the region of £35,000 to owning its own headquarters with all alterations and improvements paid for, and an increase in royalties in excess of more than 400 per cent. Although the financial position, from the company's point of view, had also improved, considering the £40,000 outlay for copyright had been made when we were in a loss-making situation, it had to be remembered that our parent company, Westminster Press, could almost certainly earn a better return on its investment from newspapers. My responsibilities were primarily to The Westmorland Gazette and, ultimately, Westminster Press. Was this in their best interests? It did not need a genius to work it out. It was not solely the financial implications. At a stroke much of the goodwill built up with AW over the past seven or eight years evaporated.

Mrs Wainwright refused to negotiate – no more TV unless the royalties were increased – so, after two or three days without any change in the position, very reluctantly I wrote to Rod Caird saying that we were not able to go ahead with the proposed TV series which we had talked about the previous week.

Retirement

AW had been working on the manuscript for the *Sixth Lakeland Sketchbook*, which he eventually delivered. Back at the office I soon realised that, because his eyesight was impaired, the usual fine detail which made his drawings so attractive was not there. After some deliberation I decided against publication. To put it on sale as a Wainwright book of drawings would be unfair to customers and would only serve to damage his reputation as an artist. Finding suitable words to give AW the news was not easy. Who was I to tell Wainwright his work was not good enough to be published? Several weeks later, when he asked how the *Sixth Sketchbook* was progressing, I had to give him my decision, explaining that the prime reason was to preserve the good reputation he had earned before his eyesight failed. It was not by any means an enjoyable experience. He went a little quiet for a few minutes but seemed to accept what I had said although he must have been disappointed.

On Monday, 10th December, 1990, Mrs Wainwright telephoned asking me to visit if I could find the time as AW wanted to see me. I was not intending to visit him that day due to commitments at the Gazette but I eventually arrived late in the afternoon. He stated that he had decided to retire. I was not surprised. His eyesight had deteriorated to .the point where he could not see to read, let alone write or draw. I still possess a book he signed for me only a week or two previously bearing a signature which indicated how poor his eyesight had become.

This was a sad day. The end of his career as an author and artist, more than 35 years since beginning work on the *Lakeland Guide Books*. I was witnessing the end of the working life of a Lake District legend. To AW it was not a particularly important event. He had never really accepted or understood the acclaim in which he was held. He said he did not wish to do any interviews but understood I would need to make an announcement for publication. I asked if he would agree to a dinner funded by The Westmorland Gazette to mark the occasion but he would not hear of it. He said: 'All I want is four Cornettos paid for by the Gazette and sometime you and I will go to the Little Chef to celebrate and I will buy you a pancake.' Unlike the usual AW he reminisced a little. We went over some matters which had occurred at various times over the past years, some of which we still disagreed over. He conceded nothing, nor did I. There was no pointing of the pipe as was usual when he was indicating the importance of whatever he was saying, no roaring, no leaning forward in the chair. He was in a relaxed mood. As he had said a short while earlier, he had retired. He reminisced about when his first book was published and he went out with the printer seeking sales outlets on a 'sale or return' basis. He enquired about David and Paul, the sons of my daughter Linda who had died nine months earlier, and about my wife's cough. He also asked how much our house was worth now and commented that we would be foolish to move from such a nice spot adding that it would be difficult to find anywhere else so well situated. Last topic was the Westmorland Heritage Plaques I was planning, utilising the letterpress printing plates used to print the limited edition of 1,000 signed and numbered copies, published in 1975.

He was not particularly confident about the plaques but was pleased when I said more than 80 had already been reserved.

On Friday, 15th December, I took his Cornettos to his house and agreed we would go to the Little Chef for his retirement lunch the following week. As we were leaving the Little Chef after the lunch he stopped outside the door and said: 'Did you enjoy that?' I replied: 'It was very good.' His response was: 'Should we go back and have another?' I don't think he was joking.

Following the announcement of his retirement, as expected there were many telephone calls from newspapers, radio and television stations etc., all requesting interviews. Initially he had indicated no interviews but now agreed to one and it had to be Eric Wallace, of Border Television. You can imagine Eric's delight when he received the news.

His Last Chapter

FRIDAY, 28th December, 1990. Nothing really important to discuss other than to let him know arrangements had been made for him to speak to Bob Smithies, of Granada Television, on Thursday, January 3rd, in The Westmorland Gazette bookstore. The arrangement was provisional because he had recently spent several days under observation in Kendal Green Hospital which was only about 300 yards from his home. He had been given a separate room off the main ward which was probably the only way he would have been prepared to be admitted knowing his attitude towards privacy. Kendal Green was a small, informal hospital where visiting was allowed at any reasonable time so I was able to call in at our usual meeting times. However, on the third visit I was in for a shock. As I entered his room expecting him to be sitting there . . . no AW, bed empty and made up. I had no idea he had been so ill. It must have been very sudden. Why had Mrs Wainwright not telephoned me? Had it just happened? All this went through my mind in the half-a-minute or so as I stood there in the doorway before a nurse appeared and asked if she could help. I said I had called to see Mr Wainwright but at that point a voice boomed, 'I'm here,' from a bed with curtains drawn around it in the main ward. He had been moved to free the separate room for someone who had passed away during the night. Recently, a nurse who worked on that ward told me that although smoking was not allowed smoke could regularly be seen rising above the curtains around his bed. That sounded exactly like AW. After he had been discharged I visited him at home where I found him in a chair by the fireside with a blanket around his shoulders. Mrs Wainwright said he was not very well and unable to keep warm. Although he appeared to be slightly drowsy he had a coffee and asked me about the last few days' football results. He could not see to read them in the newspapers and had not heard them on the radio while he was in hospital. Mrs Wainwright said that if he did not improve in the next hour or so she would call the doctor. I left at 11.25am saying I would see him again on the following Monday. I telephoned Mrs Wainwright at 4.30pm to enquire how he was but there was no reply. During a telephone conversation with her later in the evening she said he had been re-admitted to Kendal Green and she suspected he had suffered a slight stroke. He had been able to grip her hand slightly, shortly before she left the hospital. I said I would call in to see him the following afternoon, Saturday, 29th. He was discharged again during the morning of Friday, 4th January, 1991. I visited him during the afternoon and stayed with him for an hour or so while Mrs Wainwright did some shopping in Kendal. She did not want him to be left alone. His speech was very slightly affected. We were upstairs in his office which was convenient for the bathroom. While we drank coffee made by Mrs Wainwright before she went shopping I sensed he was bored and would not wish to go on living if he was to be an invalid. He reminisced a little, which was not like him. He rarely dwelt on the past. Conversations with AW were usually about what he was planning. When he had finished something it was hardly mentioned again. The *Guide Books* were a perfect example - once completed they were in the past. He said he had missed the last few episodes of *Coronation Street* while in hospital and asked if I could bring him up to date. At one point he picked up a magnifying glass and asked me if it was my coffee. He was unable to find his matches which were on the table in front of him. While bringing him up to date on events in *Coronation Street* I mentioned that in the last episode Ken Barlow had attempted to commit suicide. 'How did he go about that?' he asked. Mid-evening, probably about 8pm, Mrs Wainwright telephoned me at home to say AW was wanting to go to bed but couldn't get out of the armchair in the bedroom, could I help? I said I would go straight over but since I had had back problems for more than 20 years was unsure how I could get him onto his feet. AW was a big chap. He was sitting in the armchair with a blanket over his knees and asked if I could pull him out. As I have said before, he was at least six feet two inches and about 16 stone. The only conclusion that I came to was to stand astride of his legs, put my arms under his, clasp my hands behind his back and heave, hoping at the same time my back would stand up to it. I told him what I was going to do and he removed the blanket and lifted his arms. It worked first time. I helped him to the bed and left telling Mrs Wainwright not to hesitate if she needed me again. I sensed he had serious problems.

My next visit was due to be on the following Monday at the usual time of 2.30pm but, shortly after arriving at the office at 9am, Mrs Wainwright telephoned to say during the night she had called the doctor and at about 5am and AW had been admitted to Westmorland County Hospital with breathing problems. He was wearing an oxygen mask and although he was aware that she was there he was 'very poorly'. I was welcome to visit for a few minutes if I wished but I thought it was better for him to have complete rest. She thought it wise for us to 'keep it to ourselves'. Another telephone call on the Tuesday morning was to tell me that AW was seriously ill due to heart failure and that the next 48 hours were critical. She had spent the night at the hospital and would be going back after she had spoken to me. At 7.25pm she telephoned to say he had 'held his own' that day and, so long as his condition did not deteriorate, she would go home at about midnight, have a bath, sleep at home and go back to the hospital first thing next morning.

Over the next few days there was a slight improvement but on Sunday, 14th January he began to refuse medication. Mrs Wainwright said that the first printed flat sheets from *Wainwright in the Limestone Dales*, the book he had originally insisted Julian was to do the photography for, due to be published by Michael Joseph, had arrived and she had laid them on the floor at his bedside but he was not interested. On the following day, armed with the cheques for his royalties for the previous six months' sales, I decided to visit him. Normally he looked forward to receiving the cheques and I hoped it would cheer him up a little, especially as the results were good. I found him conscious, lying on his left side but very weak. As Mrs Wainwright had forecast he showed little interest. The visit was a mistake so far as I was concerned. AW was a few inches taller than me and

I was usually looking up to him, now he was lying down and I was looking down on him, it seemed disrespectful. While I was trying to find a suitable topic for conversation he caught me unawares with the last words I heard him speak: 'Am I dying?' Normally I have a good memory but, to this day, almost 19 years later, I cannot recall my reply. I know I tried to find a reassuring answer but have a strong feeling that it was not very convincing. It was no good. I had to leave in case he persisted with the conversation. That was the last time I was to see him. He died a week later. His last chapter had ended.

The telephone was ringing as I entered my office the morning after his death. I had arrived earlier than usual because I knew it was to be a busy day. A formal announcement about AW's death had been prepared in advance. I had anticipated for several weeks that this was 'his last chapter' and that in death, as in life, he would not want anything other than a minimum of information to be released to the media. Preferably AW would not have wanted any publicity but would have reluctantly agreed that something of a formal announcement was inevitable.

The response to the news was overwhelming. I spent most of the next three days answering telephone calls from newspapers, radio stations, television stations, etc. I think every branch of the media wanted information about AW and they were not prepared to accept the brief formal announcement. I suspect many of them had previously prepared lists of questions. It had been almost impossible over the years I worked with him to get him to accept how well known and respected he had become. The response to his first television interview had been enormous but it was nothing compared to the media interest in his death from all around the world. *The Washington Post*, in the

USA, spent more than half-an-hour on the phone seeking to know every last detail.

AW was cremated at Lancaster and Morecambe Crematorium and, in keeping with his wishes, his ashes were scattered on Haystacks.

The rest, as they say, is history. The general printing department had already been sold to Titus Wilson, of Kendal, in the late 1980s hence their name as printers on various Wainwright titles. Talks with Michael Joseph, the publisher of the glossy, coffee-table books, with photography by Derry Brabbs, took place at the head office of Penguin Ltd., in London, prior to transfer of the copyright and remaining book stocks, which, apart from the *Guide Books*, were to cease publication. Printing of the *Guide Books* was soon to be carried out overseas.

More recently, after the copyright had been returned to Mrs Wainwright, a new publisher, Frances Lincoln, emerged and adopted the *Guide Books,* revised by Chris Jesty, while also gradually re-introducing the titles which had been discontinued. Revision of the *Lakeland Guide Books* was first suggested by Chris Jesty in a letter to AW in 1980. AW politely agreed some revision was desirable but he would prefer it was left until after his death.

Prior to 1982, it was his wish that, on his death, publication of his books was to cease and all original pages and drawings which were stored in filing cabinets at the Gazette offices destroyed. Thankfully, after his death Mrs Wainwright had them transferred to the County Archives on loan. More recently it was reported that Cumbria County Council has had the opportunity to purchase the archive after securing a grant from the Heritage Lottery Fund plus support from the Friends of the National Library and Frances Lincoln Publishers.

AW will undoubtedly find his place in the folklore of the Lake District along with Beatrix Potter, William Wordsworth, John Ruskin and other literary giants. Despite the difficulties and frustrations, I feel fortunate to have spent so much time with him both as part of my employment and socially. I was not a friend of AW's simply because AW did not have friends. I think associate is more appropriate. He could have existed quite contentedly without other humans so long as there was a means of obtaining food. An otherwise uninhabited Lake District with a fish and chip shop would have been his Utopia. Regular supplies of Three Nuns tobacco would also be a requirement.

Random Reminiscences

RON Scholes, a keen fell walker from north Staffordshire who AW had introduced me to late in 1982, telephoned to enquire if I would be available to accompany AW for a meal with a party of 18 fell walkers at a restaurant at Oxenholme. As the date coincided with me being away on holiday I politely declined and was surprised when AW agreed. This was only a matter of months after he had changed his mind about having a meal at the Langdale Timeshare restaurant with whoever turned out to be the purchaser of the millionth book. Ron told me that no one bothered AW during the meal as they were expecting to be able to ask a few questions afterwards, only to be outmanoeuvred when AW stood up after his pudding and said he would have coffee at home.

HIS ancient typewriter needed the ribbon changing. Mrs Wainwright was away and I was not familiar with typewriters.

Mrs Cooke, the Gazette order clerk for the books, agreed to visit him to change the ribbon which she did but there was not even an acknowledgement when she arrived or a thank you when she left.

ALTHOUGH diminutive in comparison to AW, on the rare occasions Mrs Wainwright's patience ran out, more often than not it was he who sounded the retreat. While he was a master with the pen it was Mrs Wainwright who was in command when it came to the verbals.

ALTHOUGH he had such a high regard for animal welfare, apart from Totty, his favourite cat, I never saw AW show the slightest affection towards animals. He would sit elsewhere rather than disturb one of their nine cats but never stroked dogs or cats. After acquiring Kapellan for Animal Rescue he would spend his time there in the static caravan smoking his pipe while others walked and fed the dogs.

PRIOR to succeeding Harry Firth I had noticed a lot of small burn holes in the front passenger seat of his car. He told me they were from AW's pipe. When I later succeeded Harry I took the precaution of buying seat covers. Many of AW's clothes were also affected.

AW WAS in the habit of visiting an old friend in Blackburn and attending one of the Rovers' home matches. After his eyesight had failed he mentioned about going to Blackburn to attend a match. I was surprised as he would not be able to see the action on the pitch. He replied that he would still go because he enjoyed the atmosphere and would know the score from the reactions of the crowd.

SEVERAL universities offered AW an Honorary Degree. He replied to each one asking whether or not they carried out experiments on live animals. If they did he would decline their offer. So far as I know, all were turned down.

ABOUT a year before he died AW told me he had changed his will and it consisted of only a few words. I cannot remember the exact wording but it was something to the effect 'I leave everything I own to my wife, Betty'.

AFTER a few months of visiting on Mondays and Fridays, to save AW having to get up from his chair to open the door, Mrs Wainwright suggested I used the rear door which was unlocked and I would be able go straight in. I was never happy just knocking and walking straight in to someone else's home but did so until, on one occasion, a rather loud difference of opinion was taking place. I retreated and stood outside for a few minutes before re-entering with an equally loud, 'It's only me'. Future visits found me reverting to knocking at the front door.

ALTHOUGH he was eventually totally blind his hearing remained exceptionally good. While Ken Shepherd, a local photographer, was taking photographs of him in Langdale in the late 1980s, using time exposure, AW could hear the 'click' of the camera from something like ten feet away.

BY 1983, AW and Animal Rescue had raised about half of the amount required to buy a property suitable for the needs of the charity. I took a telephone call from a representative of a pet food manufacturer offering £5,000 in return for being allowed to use the Wainwright name to promote its product for a year. I replied that it was unlikely he would agree but promised to discuss it with him. The offer was then increased to £10,000. The response from AW was no more than an immediate slight shake of the head, hardly noticeable. Several minutes later, after dealing with the mail, he said: 'He would not be able to be sure they were telling the truth about the quality.' It was never mentioned again.

ON MONDAY, 1st February, 2010, I received a telephone call to say that the number one copy of the 100 leather bound and signed copies of *Wainwright in Lakeland*, written by AW to raise funds for Abbot Hall Art Gallery and originally, priced at £50, has been sold for £2,200.

AW WANTED me to see the starting point on the beach at St Bees Head for the Coast to Coast Walk. I was not able to spare a day out of the office so we made it a Saturday accompanied by our wives. His suggestion to paddle before beginning the walk was politely declined. Since I was not doing the walk I was not entitled to the pleasure of the paddle. On the return journey, with AW in the front passenger seat which he always claimed, he asked me to slow down slightly and pull into a lane about half-a-mile ahead, on our right. So I pulled into the side of the road, switched off the ignition and was about to ask him why when he half-turned in his seat and called to our wives: 'Andrew wants an ice cream.' There was a van parked a few yards away and AW rarely missed the opportunity to have an ice cream. What intrigued me was that, by this time (I would say either late 1988 or early 1989) he was virtually blind yet he asked me to slow down and said to watch for the little lane half-a-mile further on. His eyesight was so poor he would walk with a hand on my shoulder because he couldn't see steps, kerbs etc. After our ice creams I said to him: 'Back there you asked me to slow down and watch for the little lane on our right, I thought you couldn't see?' His response was: 'No, I can't see but I always know where I am. If you look over to your right now you will see . . .' He mentioned several mountains and said that in the slight gap and I would be able to see Haystacks. Amazing!

WE WERE invited to join AW and Mrs Wainwright for a week's holiday at Durinish, in Wester Ross, in the late 1980s, where they regularly rented a chalet. Under normal circumstances I would have made the journey in one day but, on Mrs Wainwright's insistence, an overnight stop at North Ballachulish was arranged with an evening meal in the hotel dining room. AW was not happy. Hotel dining rooms with carpets on the floor and table cloths were not his style. It was obvious he was not comfortable. Hardly a word was spoken during the meal and shortly afterwards he said he would have an early night. A fish and chip supper eaten in the car would have been more to his liking. The rest of the week we ate at the local Working Men's Club where there were no carpets or table cloths but the food was good and reasonably priced. He was perfectly happy there. His eyesight had started to fail although he wasn't completely blind at that stage. During a sight-seeing trip he wanted me to see a settlement from the 16th or 17th century where there were still a few of the old dwellings remaining. It was 'a little way further along you will come to a narrow track on the right, turn in there'. After turning in we drove along for probably two miles until the track ran out. He said he couldn't understand why we had not come to a hut that was along there. He asked me to go back again but still no sign of a hut. Mrs Wainwright asked how long since he last saw it and, after some thought, replied 11 years. Mrs Wainwright suggested he had got the wrong track but no, he was sure it was along here somewhere and asked me to go along again and he would tell me where to pull in. I did so and as we were putting our boots on to walk, a small van also pulled in and the driver opened the back doors to let two sheepdogs out. AW asked if there used to be a hut somewhere along this track and got the reply: 'Aye but a few years ago the roof blew off in the gales and I didn't use it so I pulled it down, it was there where your car is parked.'

IT WAS only a matter of weeks after the Scottish series had been aired on television that he took us to see the ancient broch which was featured in one of the episodes. As we approached the broch AW was a yard or two behind me and I overheard a lady sitting to my right say to her husband who was standing: 'This is where Mr Wainwright sat on the television programme.' As she looked up there he was, only a few feet away. Her face lit up and her voice trailed away. It was remarkable the effect he had on people. The same week we went to a small harbour he wanted me to see where the Army was carrying out some work. As we went down the hill towards the harbour we had to stop at traffic lights. At the front of the traffic, waiting to come in the other direction, was a Mercedes and I suspected the driver had recognised AW, again in the front passenger seat. The lights changed and we drove down to the harbour, parking in a small car park a short distance before the sea. As we walked out of the car park the Mercedes pulled in and was still there with its two passengers when we returned about half-an-hour later. There was no doubt he had been recognised. Depending upon the circumstances it was sometimes best not to mention that I thought he had been recognised. If it was by one of a coach load (as had happened on our journey north) it was a matter of taking evasive action but this seemed a harmless instance, at least up until now. Back up the hill we parked again in another, larger car park. We had an hour or so to kill before going to a restaurant Mrs Wainwright wanted to visit, somewhere a bit more presentable and upmarket than the local Working Men's Club where we had eaten the last few evenings. The helpings had been generous and reasonably priced but Mrs Wainwright was on holiday and was demanding a treat. Bearing in mind the little appreciation he showed in return for the way she waited on him, I felt she was entitled to a posh meal. It was an ideal spot to park with a seat at the other side of the road and beautiful views looking over to the Five Sisters of Kintail. A minute or two later the Mercedes appeared again and parked about 20 yards away. The driver obviously wanted to meet AW and was being very discreet. He must have known AW did not like being accosted and people fussing over him. I had not mentioned anything to AW about being followed or he would have wanted to drive off and we had already had a long drive that day. I was confident there was no need to worry on this occasion. After about 15 minutes I said I would join our wives on the seat leaving AW in the car. Sure enough as soon as AW was alone the driver approached our car and had a word with him. It was only for about 30 seconds then he returned to the Mercedes and drove off. When I went back to the car AW said that while I was on the seat a chap had come and thanked him for all the pleasure he had had from using the guide books for many years. 'A very polite chap,' he said. We later went on to the promised 'upmarket restaurant'. It was not what Mrs Wainwright had been expecting. It was more AW's type of place. As we waited to be served a chap in walking gear with a rucksack on the floor was sitting at the next table. Mrs Wainwright made some conversation with him and tried to involve AW, but he wasn't having any. He just wanted his meal and to get back to the chalet and, anyway, it was *Coronation Street* night. He could be obstinate if he was in that frame of mind - and he certainly was that night, refusing even to speak to the walker.

WHILE doing the walks for the Howgill Fells guide book he had often eaten in a restaurant in Sedbergh before going home in the evenings and suggested we all go there sometime. He liked the place and the food was good with generous helpings. It was a cold winter's night and as we were the only customers the owner brought an electric fire near to our table. It was so cold we kept our overcoats on. He ordered his usual fish, chips and mushy peas and I ordered a grill. Our wives' orders did not include chips. He was served first with his fish on his plate in front of him and a large bowl of chips placed in the centre of the table for us to share. He helped himself to chips, put the bowl back in the centre of the table and started to eat. Next, my grill was served and I also helped myself to chips and was replacing the bowl when he grabbed it and emptied the rest of the chips on to his plate. Obviously, because they had been brought at the same time as his fish he had thought they were all for him. Mrs Wainwright explained that because I had a grill the bowl of chips was to share but he was not very happy. I was often impressed with AW's vocabulary but I don't think it included the word hygiene. As he lifted the bowl to empty the rest of the chips onto his plate one fell onto the floor but it was not wasted. AW leaned down, picked it up and ate it.

DURING my early visits to his house, after dealing with whatever mail there was and he had made tea or coffee, he would often take two rich tea biscuits from his cardigan pocket. One each. Not the most hygienic place to put biscuits. On one occasion, as he took the biscuits out of his pocket his handkerchief fell out of the same pocket. Now AW was a pipe smoker and he certainly did not have a clean handkerchief every day, in fact probably not every week. I won't dwell on it but needless to say after that day I did not bother with a biscuit.

WHILE AW could be quiet and inoffensive there was the side of him which earned a reputation for being grumpy. I have heard of several people who refused to have anything further to do with him after being offended by his manner. Mrs Wainwright waited on him hand and foot and that was what he had come to expect. However, he could suddenly belittle her regardless of whoever else was present. As I followed him into their living room one Friday morning, two friends of Mrs Wainwright were at the other side of the room having coffee. I said 'good morning', sat down in my usual spot and started to deal with the mail when AW suddenly said out loud: 'Can you hang on until we get some privacy, these two will be going in a minute.'

AW HAD decided to retire as an author. His eyesight had gone and he decided to call it a day. As I was about to leave one day he said: 'Let me know when you can spare the time and I will take you to the Little Chef at Ings for lunch to celebrate my retirement.' I thanked him and said I would. It was a few days later when I was free at lunchtime and arranged to collect him about 12.30pm. When I arrived he called to Mrs Wainwright, who was upstairs, to bring his shoes from the kitchen, which was just as near to him as the door from which he had called her. Nevertheless, down she came, brought his shoes from the kitchen and he sat down lifting a foot up for her to put them on. She asked where we were going and he replied the Little Chef at Ings. Mrs Wainwright replied: 'Why didn't you warn me? I'm not ready.' His response was: 'This is my treat for Andrew to celebrate my retirement. I am paying for this. You are not coming.' It was most embarrassing. I could only walk outside and wait in the car. Recently on television I heard someone describe AW as quietly spoken, gentle and good-natured. Yes, he could be quietly spoken and polite but anyone who knew him well was aware of his other side.

I HAD persuaded AW and Mrs Wainwright to join us for a meal at a very good restaurant at Shap. On arrival, the procedure was to have an appetiser before being called into the dining room when the meals were ready. The proprietor took our orders and went to bring our drinks. There was a group of about half-a-dozen ladies at the other side of the room, obviously a party, who laughed out loud at something one had said. It wasn't for more than a couple of seconds but AW bellowed: 'It sounds like it is going to be a noisy night, should we go?' It was uncalled for and I am sure it put a dampener on their evening. That was his minus side. On his plus side, when my wife's mother was staying with us she joined ourselves and the Wainwrights for an evening meal. She was a few years older than AW and he was courteous enough to stand until she was seated at the table. A nice gesture.

WHEN it came to fish and chips, as far as AW was concerned distance was no object. On the outskirts of Durham City there was a fish and chip shop which was run by the third generation of the same family. In conversation I mentioned that while visiting relatives we had eaten there and the food was excellent. I should have known better. There was an immediate 'when are we going?' response. It was a round trip of more than 180 miles, we ate in the car and drove back. On another occasion while on a caravan holiday near Whitby, my wife and I found a restaurant where the fish and chips were particularly good. Again, on mentioning it, he wanted to go and sample them. Fortunately I was due to visit a book wholesaler in Scarborough so an extra journey was not necessary. On the way home from

Scarborough, he said he knew a little café in Thirsk where we could get a good cream tea. The lunch we had enjoyed in Whitby would have sufficed for me but not for AW, he had to stop for a cream tea.

ON A visit to the Kirkby Stephen area, AW enquired whether I had ever been to the Tan Hills Inn. I had, many years before when I was a lad and keen on bike riding. Together with some pals we went there for a ride out one Sunday. Too young to go in at that time it was a case of go there, turn around and head home. Today he thought we should have a ride up there and have a sandwich. On arrival, as was usual by this time, he needed the 'little boys' room' as he used to call it. The bar was very busy but I managed to find two seats next to a chap with his head in a copy of *Pennine Way Companion*, walking boots on, rucksack on the floor and completely absorbed. I got our drinks and sat down purposely leaving the seat next to the walker chap for AW, thinking this will be interesting when the chap realises who is sitting next to him. It was after the six half-hour programmes on his *Lakeland Guide Books* had been televised so there was no doubt he would recognise him. We sat there for about half-an-hour eating our sandwiches but the walker was totally occupied with the book and never looked up. Thinking it was a pity if this chap, who was probably in his late twenties, had been within touching distance of the 'Great Fellwanderer' and author of *Pennine Way Companion* without knowing, I whispered to AW that he should ask him how the walk was going. I thought it would be a nice surprise for the chap and would probably put a spring in his step for the rest of the journey but there was no response. Shortly afterwards the chap also visited the 'little boys' room', picked up his rucksack and *Pennine Way* and left the pub, none the wiser. If only he had known.

WE WERE invited to the BBC studios in Newcastle for a preview of a programme. Accompanied by our wives we went via Penrith and Hexham, stopping on the outskirts of Newcastle for directions to the studios. Pulling over to ask the way from a lady pedestrian, I realised she had recognised him. She was obviously delighted but he kept looking straight ahead. A polite 'thank you' would have made her day but that was not AW's style. He did not like being recognised and avoided conversations with strangers. It was a similar story when we arrived at the studios. I went in first, followed by AW. It was a large reception area with the enquiries desk at the other side. I went over and asked the lady if she would let Richard Else, the producer of the programmes, know that Mr Wainwright had arrived. She too had spotted him and was obviously mesmerised with his presence. Somehow she managed to pick up the telephone and press a number without taking her eyes off him. I never knew what the attraction was but he had that effect on people, probably more so women than men. It certainly was not because he was smartly dressed. As ever, it was cap with hair sticking out (which was long overdue for a trim) and his anorak. However, there was one rare occasion when he wore a suit for a visit to London – when he received his MBE. I hope Her Majesty realised how honoured she was.

To end this book, I have included two instances of the regard in which AW was held by the members of the fell walking fraternity – one very sad, the other very pleasant.

A Very Brave Young Lady...

A telephone call in 1988 from a young lady in Kent was to enquire whether it was possible to obtain a signed copy of one of AW's books. Any book, it did not matter which, so long as it contained his signature. I could not promise anything but took her telephone number and said I would return her call if AW would oblige. When a suitable opportunity arose I was able to raise it with him and he agreed. Returning the call I said I was reluctant to risk the book in the post and was pleased to hear, together with her husband, she would collect it in the near future. On their arrival, I passed the book to her. She opened it to the page bearing the signature and then handed it to her husband who spent a short while looking at the signature before a single tear fell onto his cheek. I gave them a tour of the printing works to see the various stages of the books in production before wishing them well for the future and saying goodbye. Several months later a letter arrived from the husband expressing his appreciation for obtaining the signature his wife had requested and recalled the happy visit to collect the book. However, he was sorry to tell me that his wife had, after a long illness, recently died, aged 32. Apparently she was fully aware of her terminal illness when she asked for something signed by AW but gave no indication during their visit - in fact she had been bright and pleasant. Obtaining the signature for her husband, it seemed, had been something of a last wish. Her name was Linda.

...and a Very Happy One

I was called to the Gazette shop to meet a lady, mid thirties, with a strong Irish accent and a distinctive white streak in her hair. She was also hoping it would be possible to obtain a book signed by AW. It was the same day we had launched our Presentation Pack of the *Seven Lakeland Guide Books* and a sample pack was displayed on the counter. I gave the usual response that when I thought he might agree I would ask him. As she showed an interest in the sample presentation pack I enquired if she would purchase all seven *Guide Books* if I could persuade him to sign each one? 'Yes, that would be lovely.' A few days later I phoned and said they had been signed and were ready to collect the next time she was in Kendal. A short while later they were collected by a very pleased lady with the distinctive white streak in her hair. A few months after retiring, when walking across the forecourt of our local petrol station, I heard a voice calling: 'Mr. Nichol, Mr. Nichol.' On turning around I recognised her immediately from the white streak. 'Can you wait a minute? I would like to introduce you to my husband. I knew he would marry me if I got Mr Wainwright's signature.' Remarkable the effect this Wainwright fellow had on people.